HOW TO CONDUCT

CW01010983

In this Series

CONDUCT STAFF
APPRAISALS

A practical handbook for every manager today

Nigel Hunt

How To Books

Author's dedication
To my parents, Beryl and Charles

British Library Cataloguing-in-Publication data
A catalogue record for this book is available from the
British Library.

First published in 1992 by How To Books Ltd, Plymbridge House,
Estover Road, Plymouth PL6 7PZ, United Kingdom.
Tel: Plymouth (0752) 735251/695745. Fax: (0752) 695699. Telex: 45635.

Typeset by Kestrel Data, Exeter
Printed and bound in Great Britain by
The Cromwell Press Limited, Melksham, Wiltshire

Contents

List of Illustrations

Preface

Staff appraisal has received increasing attention over the last few years, with growing awareness in organisations of the value of human recources. This book arose out of a need for a clear concise text on staff appraisal. It is aimed at anyone who carries out staff appraisals, and is intended to help individuals and organisations who are either setting up new appraisal systems, or improving existing ones.

The book does not seek to provide a blueprint for appraisal systems. There are too many individual factors involved. No two appraisal systems will be identical because no two organisations are alike. The book provides a detailed set of general guidelines from the purposes of appraisals to validating the system. The book thus provides the basic knowledge required to set up and run an effective appraisal system.

Included throughout the book are ideas from psychology that can help improve the overall standards of appraisal. These include such areas as psychometric testing and interview techniques.

I should like to express my gratitude to a number of people who have helped in the production of this book; to Richard Kerry, David Robinson and Jeremy Swinfen Green for their helpful comments on earlier drafts and, most importantly, to Jackie Barrett for her continued help and encouragement.

Nigel Hunt

1
Introduction

SUMMARY

This chapter will show how:

- Appraisal means communication between the individual and the organisation. It encompasses a broad range of situations.

- Appraisals are often poorly designed, over- or under-ambitious, and inadequately resourced.

- Effective appraisals are objective and unbiased, and take into account the needs of both the individual and the organisation.

- All workers should be appraised, from directors of large organisations to shop floor workers.

- The appraisal should be well structured, including training the participants properly, setting the objectives, preparing for the interview, the interview itself, follow up and validation.

- Appraisals should be carried out regularly, at least annually.

- Appraisals should be fair, open and promote equality and trust between the participants.

ORGANISATIONS AND APPRAISALS

An organisation's most important resource is its people. This may be a truism, but is no less valid for that. Appraisal systems should represent the best form of communication between an organisation and its people.

Appraisal can be defined in different ways. The definition used here is that is is based upon a **structured interview** that requires communication between the organisation (represented by you, the **appraiser**) and the individual employee (the **appraisee**) to make assessments about the future. But appraisal is more than just an interview; it is more broad-ranging, encompassing situations from setting performance objectives to counselling to selecting staff for promotion, transfer and training. Thus effective appraisal cannot just be a once-a-year exercise. It should be a continuous activity, with day-to-day communication between you and the appraisee.

In the formal appraisal interview, neither party should be hearing anything for the first time; problems should be broached as and when they arise. It they are left until the appraisal interview itself, they could develop from a minor problem—such as two individuals in conflict over a particular issue—to a major one where the conflict has dragged in other individuals and affected morale and productivity.

Many improvements can be made to appraisal systems as they are now often organised. They are characteristically inefficient for a number of reasons. These include:

- an unclear definition of the appraisee's job
- unclear objectives
- one or both parties being unaware of the format and aims of the interview
- untrained appraiser and/or appraisee
- subjectivity
- biased data
- incomplete data

This book attempts to address these issues in order to enable the employer to set up an appraisal system that is cost-effective to both the organisation and the employee, maximising both employee productivity and job satisfaction.

It is important that the organisation has a coherent appraisal system, and that all employees are appraised on the same system. Clearly, particular interviews will differ according to both the purposes of the appraisal and the individuals taking part, but they should all be based on the same general system so that comparisons can be made. A hotch-potch of appraisals within the organisation is inefficient, not cost-effective, and doesn't allow internal comparisons to be made.

The essential reason for an appraisal system is to ensure that the right person is in the right job, and remains in it. Maximising compatibility of person and job leads to:

- maximising personal job satisfaction
- maximising performance or output

In other words, there will be a happier, more productive workforce, which is clearly of benefit to all parties concerned.

What is wrong with appraisal?
There are many potential problems with appraisal systems. They are often poorly designed, over-ambitious, inadequately resourced, or any combination of these factors. Too often they consist simply of unstructured interviews, with neither party, appraiser nor appraisee, being fully aware of the purposes of the interview.

In these circumstances there is little point in carrying out the appraisal, as very little or no useful information will be gained from it. If the interview has no direction, no purpose, then how can either party expect to achieve anything? If this type of appraisal is the norm, the organisation may stop formal appraisals altogether because they see little benefit to be gained from them. They would be right.

An appraisal system should incorporate a number of elements for it to be effective. What follows is an attempt to describe them. This book will *not* provide a blueprint which, if followed to the letter, will ensure effective and valid appraisals; individuals and organisations differ too much for that. Nevertheless, you will be led through a series of steps that, if followed in general terms, should produce an effective system. This book should be seen as a set of guidelines which, when designing your own appraisal system and acting as appraiser, you should follow but will need to reinterpret for your own particular circumstances.

The need to be objective
A good appraisal system has to take into account the needs and wishes of both the individual being appraised and the organisation for which he or she works. There is a strong need for objectivity and lack of bias in the collection of data to be used for discussion within a well-structured appraisal interview. Too often the characteristics and requirements of the job are not known by you, the person doing the appraising. How can you judge the effectiveness of an appraisee when you do not properly understand the job itself?

WHY SHOULD YOU APPRAISE?

The employer's viewpoint
Appraisals are carried out for a number of reasons. Well designed, they will help the organisation to:

- assess the performance of individuals
- set individual objectives
- assess how well objectives are being attained
- confirm what jobs/tasks are actually being done
- determine who should be promoted or transferred
- determine who needs training and of what sort
- assess who should be considered for advancement.

The employee's viewpoint
The appraisee may see the appraisal interview differently. Unfortunately, the appraisal so often seems something to be feared. Many appraisees feel that it is carried out in order to find out who to dismiss. While this may sometimes be the case (albeit rarely), the organisation usually has different purposes in mind. If the appraisal interview is well designed, the individual should see it as:

- a career development exercise
- a way of assessing career and other wants and needs, and how the organisation can provide them
- a way of clarifying the job (duties, objectives, etc)
- a way of becoming aware of their own potential, and how that potential can be fulfilled.

This last objective may lead to difficulties if the organisation cannot fulfil this potential, because the individual, if dissatisfied, may go elsewhere. But this can be beneficial for both parties; for the individuals because they obtain greater job satisfaction by moving to another organisation, and for the organisation because it doesn't want dissatisfied individuals on its staff. Dissatisfied staff may perform poorly and demotivate others within the organisation.

The needs of the organisation and of the individual in appraisal need not be incompatible. If the individuals are satisfied with the organisation, they are more likely to share some of that organisation's philosophy (both person-centred and profit-centred). They will agree that everyone should be in the right post, that the organisation should maximise profits, that everyone should have the best chance to fulfil their potential.

Objections to appraising

The appraisal is often seen as a chore, something ordered by the powers that be, to be got out of the way once a year (or whatever the time span is). This is an unfortunate attitude as it is hardly conducive to an effective interview. The manager who holds this opinion may claim that appraisal is carried out on a day-to-day informal basis, that problems which emerge are solved as they arise, suitability for promotion or a bonus are assessed using informal continuous assessment, etc. These managers will claim that formal appraisals are pointless as they do not provide any information not already obtained by day-to-day contact.

There are other reasons why some managers are against appraisals. For various reasons they may not actually like doing appraisals. These reasons include:

- dislike of the interview situation
- lack of time
- confrontational nature of the interview
- embarrassment if the appraisee is substandard
- hard work preparing for the interview
- not knowing how to structure the interview
- thinking they can't make accurate assessments of people.

This list isn't comprehensive. Most people could probably add a few more personal reasons for avoiding appraisal interviews.

This book should allay the fears of managers who have lists such as the one above in their minds. If the appraisal interview is designed properly, if both you and the appraisee understand the purposes and plan of the interview, if clear guidelines are given for assessing the appraisee, then perhaps managers will take a more positive attitude to appraisal. The purpose of this book is to allay the fears and quieten the protests of managers who, for one reason or another, are against appraisal interviewing. If both parties are made fully aware of the benefits of appraisal, then the traditional notion of the appraisal interview as a regular chore can be eliminated and replaced with a more positive attitude.

WHO SHOULD BE APPRAISED?

Many organisations only appraise individuals in the middle ranks.

That is, they don't appraise lower grade office staff and blue collar workers, nor their top managers. One reason is that there often exists a set format for the appraisal, and that format is not seen as being appropriate for either the higher or the lower strata of workers. While the appraisal system within an organisation should be standard, it is crucial to allow scope for different types of appraisal at different levels within the organisation.

● It is not making best use of the appraisal to give everyone within the organisation, irrespective of position and rank, the same appraisal interview and the same appraisal report.

Lower levels of staff

A common reason for not appraising lower levels of staff has to do with organisational philosophy, the artificial barriers often created between 'worker' and 'manager'. The workers lower down the hierarchy are seen as less valuable and as having less potential than those with higher rank, and it may be hard for them to get promotion. This attitude is changing now, at least in some industries, but there are still many organisations that function in this way.

Failure to appraise the lower strata of workers can lead to a waste of resources. At first sight, appraisal of workers who carry out generally routine activities may seem a waste of money, especially when performance can be judged very easily (number of letters typed, number of machine bits drilled) and without an appraisal interview. So why bother appraising this section of staff? The main reason is to ensure you are not ignoring potential within these groups.

The worker on the assembly line who has potential for promotion will find it difficult to prove this to the organisation. For one thing, assembly lines function at a particular speed, so the operative often will not even be able to show above average performance on any objective production criterion. The job is designed to be so routine there is no scope for flexibility, so the individual will not be able to display initiative in other ways. Without a well-designed appraisal system, that can in some way (not necessarily just through interviewing but also using techniques such as group exercises) demonstrate who has leadership potential, the operative who has potential will remain trapped in the wrong job. He or she may become frustrated, decrease overall productivity and leave, all because the organisation didn't provide a suitable appraisal system.

Higher levels of staff

A reason often given for not appraising the higher levels of staff is that it is hard to find someone senior enough to do the appraising. It is also harder to establish performance criteria. Many people in such positions refuse to accept appraisal, declaring that their position proves their worth to the company, and if the company doesn't accept that evidence then they will think of moving on. If this situation arises, appraisal may not be the best approach! Otherwise, even for high-ranking executives, appraisal can provide benefits. An appraisal carried out by the personnel director on the managing director can be justified in terms of authority. Even though the personel director may be lower in rank, he has authority as head of personnel.

Older staff

Another group that can be left out of the appraisal process is older workers. It is often assumed that someone who has passed 50 has peaked and is too old to be considered for transfer, promotion or training. This is a wrong assumption. In the modern world there are ever greater numbers of people who are changing jobs and organisations more often and later in life. It is no longer the norm to stay with the same organisation throughout one's working life. A 50-year-old person may still have 15 years of work left before he or she retires, possibly more. To be able to make use of such knowledge and experience, and perhaps adapt them to new roles, may be very beneficial to the organisation. But the organisation cannot assess whether that person is suitable for retraining or transfer unless he or she is appraised.

People represent a financial investment, and that investment is not always fully utilised. Appraisal, at all levels, is a way of ensuring that the investment in human resources is more efficiently used.

HOW AND WHEN SHOULD YOU APPRAISE?

How to appraise

There are a number of stages to consider regarding the structure of the appraisal, the appraisal itself, and the follow-up:

1. Both you and the appraisee should be trained in appraisal techniques, eg: **interviewing, negotiation, counselling**. It is crucial that you both have the appropriate skills, so that you can interact on a similar level in the interview.

2. You should decide why the appraisal is to be carried out. For example: to **set performance objectives, assign rewards/ punishments, determine training needs, promotion, transfer, selection, redundancy, vocational guidance, future potential, job redesign,** or a combination of some of these factors in the form of a regular review.

3. You decide what **data** to collect for the appraisal, eg: **performance criteria, supervisor ratings,** and consider how the data can be collected.

4. You talk to the appraisee to discuss the forthcoming appraisal, its purposes, and to let the appraisee make suggestions as to content. Any changes to the purposes of the appraisal can then be made.

5. The data is collected. This data should be as relevant, objective and unbiased as possible. If data is difficult to obtain then a suitable **discussion document** can be prepared.

6. When the data has been collected, it is summarised in a **report** made available to both you and the appraisee. The information should be understandable to both parties. Any complex analyses should be fully explained.

7. The appraisee is given time to digest the report and come up with **discussion points** arising from it.

8. The appraisal interview itself can take place. You should have designed the interview carefully, planning it so that all relevant points can be discussed. These can arise from assessing the appraisee's previous objectives and success at attaining them, from the report, from discussion points the appraisee wishes to raise, and from negotiation, where the two parties agree on the appraisee's future **objectives**.

9. **Appraisal report**. This can be written up by yourself or by the appraisee, and should include information on points discussed, conclusions reached and objectives set. It should be signed by both parties to say that they agree with the content. There will also be space for the other party to add comments. This report ensures that no one can later dispute the agreements reached.

10. **Follow up**. It is important that whatever was promised in the appraisal interview is actually provided. If you promised a certain type of training, then that training should be given.

When to appraise

When there are appraisals for measuring performance against objectives, perhaps based on training, they must be carried out regularly, at least annually and, if appropriate and practical, more often. In this way continuity of assessment is ensured. An effective appraisal can be a good motivator to a good employee, so it is worth doing regularly. There doesn't have to be a reason for the appraisal apart from a simple check on performance objectives: have they been reached? If not, why not? What new objectives should be set?

There are good reasons for appraising individuals at other times. These include:

- if a promotion becomes available
- after a probationary period for new employees
- after promotion or transfer
- when introducing new responsibilities
- after disciplinary procedures.

ETHICAL CONSIDERATIONS

Appraisal raises questions of fairness, openness, equality and trust. Fairness relates to the way different appraisees are treated. Openness refers to allowing both yourself and the appraisee access to all information that is going to be used in the appraisal (though this may not always be possible). Equality refers to the equality of yourself and the appraisee as to your respective roles in the appraisal interview itself, rather than your status within the organisation. Trust refers to the confidentiality that must be respected in the dialogue.

Fairness

All individuals within the organisation should be treated in a similar fashion when they are being appraised. This does not mean that they must all receive the same type of appraisal, but it does mean that the same guidelines are used for designing the appraisal, carrying it out, and reaching conclusions and judgements about performance. If the data used in the appraisal are objective, and collected properly, and the appraisal interview itself is well planned, then the outcome is more likely to be fair. This subject is discussed in more detail later.

Openness

In order to carry out an effective appraisal, both parties—you, representing the organisation, and the appraisee—must as far as possible be fully knowledgeable about all the information that is to be used in the appraisal. Openness leads to honesty and trust, and openness on the part of the organisation will encourage the appraisee to express himself fully, without fearing that the organisation is hiding information.

On the whole, openness within the appraisal interview can be achieved. There are many organisations though which would disagree with that. Perhaps they think it best not to let the staff know the organisational objectives, or the overall sales figures for the previous year. Why is this? Why do they keep information from staff? Staff should be encouraged to be part of the organisation. If they know what is happening, if they know the present performance and future plans of the organisation, they are more likely to feel part of that organisation. They will then be motivated to work more effectively, and have much more job satisfaction. Openness benefits both sides, bringing more profit for the organisation and more satisfaction for the individual.

A survey has shown that 92 per cent of appraisees see some of their appraisal report, but part of the report is often still secret. There is a largely unfounded fear among managers that total openness would lead to blander, more lenient reports. Research has shown though that where appraisal reports are open, managers are just more *careful* about what they write, rather than less frank. They are more likely to obtain evidence for their position.

Equality

A sense of equality between the appraiser and the appraisee is important. The appraiser will usually be senior in rank to the appraisee, but that doesn't mean a sense of equality can't be engendered. Both parties need to be able to talk freely, to exchange ideas without fear of rebuke.

The lower-ranking appraisee

The usual situation is that you as the appraiser are of higher rank than the appraisee, and this can make it difficult for the appraisee to speak openly, especially when wishing to criticise the organisation. (This is particularly difficult if you are the appraisee's supervisor. It is suggested later that, for this reason, the appraiser should not be the immediate supervisor). In these cases it is crucial that any implied threat about speaking one's mind is removed.

The higher-ranking appraisee
The other problem of equality is one alluded to earlier, that of the appraisee being of higher rank than yourself. This problem may be eased by using the personnel director as the appraiser, though the appraisal still remains a potentially threatening situation.

The element of threat can be removed if both you and appraisee understand the reasons behind the appraisal system, its purposes, and the way it operates. You are then both more likely to accept your roles within the system, and to act appropriately. It is important that appraisees are shown *why* they should be on equal terms with you. If they see the benefits they will act appropriately.

Trust
Confidentiality is essential in appraisals. If appraisees don't believe they can trust you to act confidentially regarding whatever is discussed in the interview, then they are less likely to say what they think. For example, there may be a delicate underlying personal problem. If the appraisee can share this with you appropriate action can be taken, but if the appraisee doesn't trust you then nothing will get done and the problem will remain, and may become more serious over time.

PSYCHOLOGICAL TESTING, COUNSELLING AND NEGOTIATION

Psychological testing
Most appraisal systems make no use of psychological testing. This is unfortunate as it is one of the most important ways in which psychology can assist effective appraisal systems. There are many different tests that measure many different areas of human performance. There are **aptitude** and **ability tests** that help assess whether an individual has the right kind of abilities to do particular jobs, **personality tests** that help decide whether the individual has any characteristics that might conflict with his or her performance, and tests that assess an individual's interests. Tests are particularly useful when the appraisal is for promotion or transfer, as they are good predictors of performance in new situations. (See Chapter 4.)

Counselling skills

It is crucial that you have basic counselling skills, so that you can cope properly with personal issues and problems that emerge from the appraisal interview. An appraisee handled badly in this situation can be expensive, both in human and financial terms.

Negotiation

Basic negotiation skills are needed by both parties so that in cases of disagreement it will be easier to work out solutions to problems. Without such skills, when neither party can effectively argue their case, the appraisal may revert to dominant/subordinate roles with you imposing your will on the appraisee, for example when setting objectives for future performance. By using negotiation skills it is more likely that an arrangement fair to both parties will be arrived at.

WHAT YOU'LL FIND IN THE REST OF THE BOOK

The following chapters go through the stages of designing an appraisal, running it and following up.

- Chapter 2 considers purposes of appraisal interviews.

- Chapter 3 is concerned with how individuals should be trained to perform optimally in the appraisal interview.

- Chapter 4, 5 and 6 cover the actual preparation for the appraisal interview, from deciding who should carry out the appraisal, to determining the purposes of the appraisal, collecting and summarising relevant data, allowing both parties to suggest discussion points arising from the data, and structuring the interview.

- Chapter 7 considers the appraisal interview: when and where it should be held, the interview itself, and the appraisal report.

- Chapter 8 considers following up the appraisal interview with specific actions, and assesses the effectiveness of the appraisal system itself.

- Chapter 9 draws a number of conclusions.

Case study: Ethical issues

John Parkin is a middle manager in a medium-sized company in the South East. His responsibilities include selection and appraisal within his department. Though he has many years of managerial experience, is popular with most of the workforce and is expected to rise further in the company, John operates an implicit sexist policy. The only ones who know about this 'policy' are John's colleagues in his department and, partly perhaps because they are male, they do not consider it an issue worth protesting about.

Put quite simply, John will not employ females either in the workshop, as supervisors, or as managers. He will only employ them in clerical roles. This policy is not questioned by the company as: one, they do not operate any checking system on the categories of people employed, and two, the type of work carried out by John's department has always tended to be a male-dominated area.

John considers his appraisal system to be very efficient. There is no company-wide policy, responsibility being delegated to departmental heads. John appraises everyone regularly, he gives them adequate time for preparation, has an excellent interview technique, covers all the right issues relating to both the organisation and the appraisee and invariably follows up with appropriate action. Unfortunately, the same system doesn't apply to female members of the clerical staff. For this group, John's first (and to him most important) question is: 'When are you going to get pregnant?'.

Comment

This example illustrates how an apparently good appraisal system is rendered invalid by a single individual operating a policy that is unknown to the company (and in this case illegal). The situation would be improved by the company:

(a) adopting a companywide appraisal system that involved systematically training appraisers and ensuring they treat everyone fairly by collecting appropriate data, and

(b) because it is a traditionally male-dominated area, having a positive discrimination policy to encourage females to enter the company and to ensure that once there they are treated fairly.

POINTS FOR DISCUSSION

1. How might different individuals or groups be treated unfairly in an appraisal?

2. Consider the way you conduct appraisals at work. List the areas where your appraisal technique is (a) good, (b) may need improving. Include anything to do with the way you prepare for the interview, how you conduct the interview, and how you act on the outcome of the interview.

3. How would you go about appraising a senior director in your organisation?

2
What is Appraisal For?

SUMMARY

In this chapter we'll see how:

- The purposes of the appraisal should be clearly defined well before the interview takes place.

- There is no real conflict between the purposes of the appraisal as the employee sees it and as the organisation sees it.

- Effective appraisals should maximise performance for the organisation.

- Effective appraisals should maximise job satisfaction for the individual.

- Appraisals are used for: regular performance review, setting objectives, assigning rewards and punishments, determining training needs, promotion and transfer, selection, redundancy, vocational guidance, assessing future potential and job re-design.

One major problem with appraisals is that the participants do not know what they are for. Often their purpose is not clearly defined. They consist simply of an interview between an individual (the appraisee) and his immediate supervisor (you, the appraiser). These interviews may have some structure, or just be general chats about the appraisee's performance. They are often based on little or no objective data about the appraisee, and as such have little real value.

Another problem seems to lie in an apparent conflict between the purposes of the appraisal interview as the organisation sees them, and the purposes as the appraisee sees them. This conflict is largely imaginary, but it is reinforced and perpetuated by the behaviour of both the organisation and of the appraisee. As the appraiser, you may be keeping much of the data obtained for and from the appraisal interview secret, and the appraisee may believe the organisation is trying to catch them out and find an excuse for not giving them a full bonus, or not promoting them or, in the worst case, dismissing them.

This chapter describes the main purposes of appraisal interviews. Anyone trying to set up an appraisal system should, before doing anything else, clarify the purposes of the appraisal. This determines everything that follows, from the selection of appropriate data to designing the appraisal interview, and the conclusions to be drawn from it.

Types of appraisal interview
Never lose sight of the underlying reasons for all appraisals:

- to maximise performance for the organisation
- to maximise job satisfaction for the individual.

Remember, in a good appraisal system these are not conflicting reasons; they are complementary.

Most appraisals are carried out with a limited number of purposes in mind. It is not usually helpful or necessary to design a single system that incorporates all or even most of the following general purposes. For example, an appraisal to assess the performance of an individual new to the organisation will consider the performance of the individual to date. It will look at training needs that have emerged in the first few months, and perhaps consider future potential, possibly providing some guidance on how the career of the individual could progress over the next few years. Another type of appraisal, the regular performance review, would not necessarily consider training needs on every occasion, nor would it make use of psychological tests. Thus different appraisals cover different areas.

THE REGULAR PERFORMANCE REVIEW

This is perhaps the most common purpose of the appraisal interview. It is extremely important, as it helps to build up a picture of the performance of the organisation, and of its individual employees. It is crucial to carry out this kind of appraisal regularly. It is often done annually, but it could be carried out every six months, or even every three months. It depends on:

- the philosophy of the organisation
- the individuals involved in the appraising
- the content of the appraisal
- the cost of the appraisal (in time and money)
- the general economic situation as it affects the organisation.

With a performance review, it is important that the procedure remains largely the same year after year (apart from necessary updating of the appraisal system). This will help direct comparisons of performance over several years. Some authors have argued against this, on the grounds that if an individual had one particularly good year, then performance in the future shouldn't be blighted in contrast. By making comparisons of this sort, though, the organisation can find out why individuals who normally do well might sometimes do less well. A pattern may emerge over several reviews. Perhaps there is a gradual falling off in performance, suggesting decreasing job satisfaction, caused by boredom with doing the same job for too long. These comparisons are made possible by keeping all the performance data over the years.

Regular performance review systems, if not constantly monitored and upgraded, may become obsolete in time. This is why validation needs to be constantly carried out to check whether it is doing its job (see Chapter 8). It is a key element of any appraisal system. It is the best way of checking whether the system is working.

The regular performance review has advantages in that appraisees gradually become familiar with what it entails. They become more confident at expressing themselves in the appraisal situation. They become more willing to accept performance objectives based on the appraisal, because they themselves will be part of the decision-making process. This process can be extended, so that the appraisal enables the appraisee to make comments about how the organisation as a whole is functioning, a kind of elaborate 'suggestion box'.

OBJECTIVE SETTING

This is the traditional purpose of appraisal interviews. Basically, the appraisee's performance is assessed against previous objectives and, by mutual consent, new objectives are set for the coming year. It is crucial that objectives are agreed by both parties. The appraiser will have to ensure that realistic objectives, in management terms, are set, and the appraisee must be fully committed to the objectives in order to perform effectively. Sometimes over-zealous appraisees will need to be held back, as they may try to set over-ambitious targets for themselves.

How to set realistic objectives

Setting objectives is an important function. It concerns what the appraisee will be doing in the future. The setting of objectives should be a careful process that takes into account a number of factors, including:

- performance against previous objectives
- aptitude at job
- personal circumstances
- future potential
- the changing work environment.

Reasonable objectives give appraisees sensible guidelines against which to work for the coming year. If these guidelines aren't present, or aren't sufficiently clear, appraisees may not know what is expected from them.

Once you are in the appraisal interview, you must be in a position to discuss the objectives to be set for the coming year. Any organisation has a hierarchy of objectives, from corporate to employee. Here we need only consider the employee's, the appraisee's, objectives. What should the appraisee reasonably be expected to achieve and, very importantly, what **performance criteria** should be used?

Performance criteria

These should be chosen carefully, especially for situations where performance is not easily quantifiable. Perhaps the best example of this is management. There is little point in setting objectives that aren't measurable in terms of actual performance. For some jobs, quantifiable assessment is easy, for others it is more difficult. But for any assessment of performance the criteria chosen should be rational, allow systematic measurement, and be stable over time. Stability enables the organisation to monitor individual and organisational trends. Possible criteria include:

- direct financial indices, such as sales volume or profit;
- direct quantitative measures, such as units of production or number of customers;
- ratios, such as errors per 100 transactions or sales per 100 contacts;
- time factors, such as time it takes to complete a task, or ability to meet deadlines;
- judgemental scales, such as supervisor ratings, peer ratings, and ratings of inferiors;
- descriptive opinion.

These can be categorised into quantitative or qualitative criteria (with a gradual decrease in quantitativity as one reads down the list). Quantitative data is usually easier to obtain and analyse, but care still needs to be taken to ensure extraneous factors have been accounted for. For instance, if the criterion is 'sales volume' then account should be taken of size of sales territory, number of potential customers, number of actual customers, time spent in the field, experience, and any other factors that might have a bearing on the criterion.

Objectives and the organisation's structure
Objectives depend on the organisational structure. Does the organisation set individual targets at a level higher than the appraiser? If so you will not be able to use your negotiating skills very much because you won't have the authority to set targets. In extreme cases, you will simply have to tell the appraisee what must be achieved in the coming 12 months. Cases like this don't help effective appraisals, or good employee relations. Indeed, they should not really be considered as appraisals at all, because they involve little or no interaction between the organisation and the individual, and will not serve the crucial purpose of ensuring employee job satisfaction. There is little point in having an appraisal interview if it is only to instruct. The employee might as well be sent a letter. The point of the appraisal is to enable *discussion* to take place.

You need to know the upper and lower limits of your negotiating position, and to encourage the appraisee to accept higher objectives —but only if this is feasible based on findings revealed by the data obtained for the appraisal regarding past performance, and other matters that arise out of the appraisal procedure.

ASSIGNING REWARDS AND PUNISHMENTS

It is useful to use the appraisal system to assign rewards, whether these are pay bonuses, revised work conditions, or simply verbal praise. Punishments should also be assigned where appropriate, for example withdrawal of bonus or verbal criticism. If the performance of the appraisee has been particularly good over the period under review, then a few simple words of praise is one of the best motivators for future performance.

● *Praise is usually a better motivator than a pay bonus.*

It is easy to give regularly, when deserved, but a bonus cannot be provided every time someone performs well. If it is, then the employee comes to expect it as a matter of course. However, the best motivator for one class of workers may not be the best motivator for another. For example, praise may work well on junior management, but pay incentives may be more effective for production line workers.

The importance of reward/punishment within the appraisal system cannot be underestimated. It is crucial for most, if not all, kinds of appraisal. A major demotivator for the appraisee is to come out of the appraisal interview not having been either rewarded for good performance or punished for poor performance.

Your power to reward and punish

Your ability to mete out rewards and punishments depends on a number of factors. One factor is your status, both in relation to the appraisee and in the organisation as a whole. This factor may have effects on the relationship between the two parties in the appraisal interview itself.

If the appraisee knows you haven't a great deal of power to mete out reward or punishment, then that gives the appraisee relatively more power within the relationship.

Organisational policy may affect your ability to provide rewards and punishments. For instance, some companies provide a generous optional bonus scheme, while others do not.

The size of the organisation will also be a key factor; certain rewards and punishments may not be available to the smaller company. For instance sending your best salesman to Jamaica for a month's holiday may be beyond the budget of many companies. Market forces also play a part. In times of recession there is less money to use for rewards.

When criticism is used as a punishment, there is no advantage in the appraisee simply being told off for poor performance.

● *Criticism has to be supported by constructive comments about how to improve performance.*

Just as failure to praise in appropriate circumstances can be de-motivating, so can criticism without constructive comment.

DETERMINING TRAINING NEEDS

Employees should always have access to any training courses that will help their performance and career development. The appraisal interview can help determine training needs in a number of ways. You can:

● ask the appraisee
● ask the appraisee's supervisor
● assess flaws in performance and discuss how these might be rectified
● apply appropriate psychological tests
● look into the appraisee's record to see which courses have already been attended.

There is little advantage in sending employees on training courses without accurately assessing their particular needs. In- dividuals and jobs differ so much that off-the-peg training courses are likely to be wasteful of resources.

Instead of meting out punishments if the appraisee isn't per-forming effectively, the appraisal interview might bring out that the real reason is that the appraisee doesn't have the necessary skills. To give a simple example, the appraisee might have been given the job of negotiator for buying certain goods. In other buying functions they may have performed well, but faced with trained and experienced negotiators they are out of their depth. Without analysing the situation, you may decide to punish the appraisee in some way (eg withhold a bonus); but if you carry out the assessment properly, you will find that the appraisee simply needs training in basic negotiating skills.

Training needs can be determined in a number of ways. These will depend on the particular need, the person involved and the situation itself (organisational objectives and climate, availability of particular training courses, etc).

Asking the appraisee is useful because they are the ones who often know their job best, and can to some extent judge their own effectiveness and where their weaknesses lie. These weaknesses can often be offset by training.

The supervisor of the appraisee is also a good person to determine training needs.

Other issues may arise from the appraisal interview itself, or from the data collected for the interview. For instance, a personality questionnaire may have established that the appraisee lacks assertiveness, yet is in a role where assertiveness is a positive characteristic. If this result is discussed in the interview, and the appraisee agrees with the result of the questionnaire, then you can recommend the appraisee to go on an assertiveness course.

PROMOTION AND TRANSFER

Promotion and transfer are separate but linked purposes of appraisal interviews. They are separate in that promotion involves moving to a higher status post while transfer doesn't (and may indeed involve a demotion). The link is that both involve the appraisee moving from one post to another.

This type of appraisal involves more than an assessment of current performance and prediction of future performance in the same post, ie the basic appraisal procedure. Here judgements are made about the individual's potential to do well in a *different* role. Of course, that role may be very similar, in which case past performance may be very relevant; but where the roles are very different, the appraiser should be very careful about making judgements as to which candidate will perform best in this new role. It is unwise to assume that just because someone is doing exceptionally well at their present job they will do equally well in a new role. The new role may well involve very different job tasks and perhaps much more responsibility.

The danger of promoting someone too high, to their level of incompetence, is sometimes called the 'Peter Principle'. Clearly, if this occurs, neither the organisation nor the individual will benefit. It is likely that the organisation will lose money by having an incompetent person in a particular position, and the individual will clearly be dissatisfied trying to do a job for which they are not well suited.

The role of psychological tests

This is where psychological tests can help. Tests are very useful for helping make predictions about future performance that are not based on past performance (at least, not in the same way as a simple appraisal is). Measuring the characteristics of people already performing that new role, and finding out what it is that separates the better performers from the weaker ones, allows the appraiser to establish a template against which to measure those individuals who may be transferred or promoted to that role. (For more details on psychological testing, see Chapter 6.)

Appraisal interview as selection interview

When considering promotion or transfer, the appraisal interview takes on the role of a selection interview. The design of the interview should be altered accordingly. This is described in detail later. The appraisal may still consider previous objectives and performance, but it may not be useful to discuss *future* objectives. This is because it is still undecided who will be promoted. While it is necessary to discuss the general performance requirements of the job, there is little point in discussing particular objectives with someone who is not in that particular role. It is a waste of resources, as specific objectives set will partly depend on the person appointed. Thus a promotion appraisal should not be part of the regular performance review. It should be quite separate.

SELECTION

Selection is not usually seen as a form of appraisal, and perhaps the boundaries of the concept are being stretched a little. However, appraisal systems are part of the overall human resource management of the organisation, and so is selection. The selection process is similar in structure and content to the promotion/transfer appraisal, except that in selection the 'appraisees' are outside the organisation. In fact there is greater overlap than this, because applicants for a particular post often come from inside as well as outside the organisation. This is the main justification for including selection appraisals here.

If there are applicants from both within and outside the organisation it is fair and efficient to subject both groups to more or less the same procedure. This will include an interview that is well-structured, and based on certain types of data, such as the application form, which reveals details of skills and interests, references or supervisor ratings (depending on whether the candidate is external or internal), which give an indication of past performance (references should be obtained on a form similar to that completed for supervisor ratings), and psychological tests which are, when used correctly, the best predictors of future performance.

There will be differences in the way internal and external candidates are treated, simply because the organisation usually knows more about the internal candidate. These differences shouldn't adversely affect the selection procedure, as both types of candidate will in the end be assessed on the same person specification.

REDUNDANCY

This is probably the most difficult type of appraisal, both for yourself and the appraisee. Redundancy appraisals are carried out when the organisation, for whatever reason, has to cut back on its staff. It makes economic sense to make the least well-performing individuals redundant. These appraisals are therefore designed to assess performance (rather than optimise job satisfaction), to find out who is performing at a standard below that required, or who is doing relatively worse than other employees in similar positions. If there is little to distinguish between performance, then length of service is usually the next factor taken into account, with the general rule that those who arrive last leave first.

In this type of appraisal it is crucial that you display counselling skills (see Chapter 3), and build vocational guidance into the procedure.

Redundancy is not always the only answer to an overstaffed department. It may sometimes be possible to transfer the individual to another department.

VOCATIONAL GUIDANCE

Guidance should be provided where the individual is made redundant, whether compulsorily or voluntarily. It is fair to do so, as the situation is not brought about through any major fault in the employee, apart from having a relatively poorer performance record than other employees. There is even more reason for the organisation to help if the employee has been made redundant because of length of service.

This again goes slightly away from the usual definitions of appraisal, but it is linked. Some say that vocational guidance isn't and shouldn't be part of appraisal. But we began by saying that appraisal means ensuring the right person is in the right job, maximising both job satisfaction and productivity. If the organisation is dismissing the employee when that employee hasn't committed a misdemeanour, then the organisation is morally obliged to do all it can to help that employee find another job in which he or she will obtain maximum job satisfaction.

Vocational guidance techniques

The most effective vocational guidance involves the employee completing a series of questionnaires and psychological tests. These will provide a great deal of information about him or herself, including aptitudes, personality and interests. The right psychological tests will generate ideas for the right kinds of careers. A structured interview can be designed to explain these findings to the employee, and suggest the types of jobs that may be suitable, and how to go about obtaining further details.

The organisation should also ensure the redundant worker has all the necessary skills for obtaining another job, such as:

- curriculum vitae writing
- filling in application forms
- interview techniques.

By providing this service, the organisation goes some way to ensuring the leaving employee has a reasonable chance of obtaining a new job that will prove satisfying.

ASSESSING FUTURE POTENTIAL

Assessing future potential is not the same as an appraisal for promotion or transfer, where there is a specific vacancy available and the organisation is looking for someone to fill it. Here the purpose is to find out which employees are likely to rise through the ranks. It is also used to identify who might be suitable not necessarily for promotion, but for transfer to a different department, perhaps to do a quite different job.

High flyers

It is important to find out who is likely to be a 'high-flyer' so that they can be prepared for their future roles, which will probably involve a great deal of training. If a person seems suitable for higher management, then they can perhaps be placed on a programme of courses designed to prepare them for that kind of role. Accurate assessment is crucial in these cases because training is usually very expensive; if the wrong individual is chosen the organisation may waste a lot of money.

Transfers

Likewise, if someone looks as if they may be more suited to a different type of job within the organisation, perhaps a transfer to a different department, they should be prepared for that. This may again involve training, or perhaps a temporary transfer to see how they get on.

What data is needed?

In order to assess future potential, you will need various types of data. Past performance is not necessarily a guarantee of future performance in a different role, but that doesn't mean it is of no value. It is useful to introduce ideas from selection, even though here there is no specific job for which the appraisee is being selected.

Psychological tests again provide a useful means of assessment. Using appropriate tests you can determine the range of aptitudes and interests of the person, along with personality characteristics and motivating factors. You can build up a picture of the person, and assess how far their present responsibilities exploit these aptitudes and characteristics, and see which ones are suited to higher roles, or roles in other departments. (See Chapter 5 for details of how to determine which individual characteristics are important for which jobs.)

Using these findings as a basis for discussion, the appraisal interview can draw out further information to complete the picture, and to determine the best direction for the appraisee's career. This type of appraisal also decreases the risk of possible future job dissatisfaction. For instance, if the appraisee is not using their general intelligence to the full in their present post, then dissatisfaction is likely in the long term unless there are promotion prospects (derived from the future potential appraisal) to take them to their level of ability. The personal profile of characteristics obtained from the appraisee can also help identify training needs. If the appraisee shows a flair for a certain subject, brought out by an aptitude test, then this flair can be trained and brought into use in the organisation.

JOB REDESIGN

Appraisals are useful to help discover how jobs themselves, rather than the individuals doing them, are at fault. This is an appraisal of the *job* rather than the *person*, so again the boundaries of the concept are stretched.

Jobs are often badly structured or inappropriate. Many jobs in a lot of organisations are simply a hotch-potch of tasks, thrown together to serve a particular purpose at a certain time and built up in a relatively random manner over the years by different people taking on various tasks at different times. If the personnel department tried to analyse this kind of job they would typically fail to find any coherence. There would be no reason why these miscellaneous tasks should be put together to be carried out by one person under a single job title.

When the organisation has jobs like this, it is useful to carry out an appraisal of staff to determine their views on how the job might be designed in a more coherent way. The organisation might find that an apparently hotch-potch job is being done by a person who is perfectly happy doing that particular range of tasks, in which case it may be more efficient to leave the job as it is. Or they may find that the person doing it is immensely dissatisfied, in which case a radical job redesign may be necessary. In both cases, the importance of the appraisal is that it allows the organisation to assess the views of staff.

The appraisal interview carried out to assess the need for job redesign is more of an advice and information gathering session than one designed to assess the appraisee. Yet it still falls under the heading of appraisal because it is concerned with contact between organisation and appraisee to increase productivity and employee satisfaction.

Appraisal for job redesign is only needed rarely, and in organisations that have for some reason become inefficient because of the incoherent nature of the jobs its employees are doing. Individual job redesign appraisals may also be needed when particular employees are unhappy with the pattern of tasks they are required to do, and the appraiser will need to see whether the tasks can be redistributed in a better way. In this case much preparation for the appraisal interview is needed, to see what the options are.

INTEGRATED OBJECTIVES

These various purposes of appraisal systems are often closely linked within a single appraisal interview. They are not designed to exclude each other. Appraisal interviews should rightly concern more than one of the above categories. For instance, if you wish to carry out the regular performance review, you are likely to include an assessment of training needs, future potential, and the setting of objectives. It is more cost-effective to put them together

Case study: Performance review

Robert was being appraised with Jack, and had already covered various aspects of his performance over the last six months when Jack says:

'I'd like to turn to this problem you're having with stock levels. I hear that levels are so low you're having difficulty meeting orders on time, and that the Whitesons order was two days late. You need to make sure levels are adequate. You can't afford to be late with these orders.'

'Yes, but the problem is . . .'

Jack interrupts: 'I don't want to hear why, I just want it sorted out—quickly.' Clearly, there are a lot of problems with this interchange. A better approach would be:

Jack: 'I'd like to turn to this problem we're having with stock levels. I've been told by despatch that we're having difficulty meeting orders on time, and one order was late. Can you tell me about it?'

Robert: 'Yes, it's true I'm afraid. Stock levels had been kept down because we had been having problems with high levels. If you remember we discussed this a few months ago and agreed to decrease levels. Now we have all these extra orders production are having difficulty keeping up.'

Jack: 'Yes I see what you mean. What do you think we should do about it?'

Robert: 'Well, we're over the worst of it now, stock levels are rising again, and I think we can get the orders out on schedule. But for the future, if we had more information from marketing I don't think the problem would have arisen. We just weren't prepared for the extra orders.'

Jack: 'OK, I'll get on to marketing and make sure you get the information you need. I suppose monthly would be all right?'

'Robert: 'Yes.'

'Jack: 'What about future stock levels?'

Robert: 'If I get the right information from marketing then we can keep them down to our previously agreed figure.'

Jack: 'Right, we'll give it a try.'

Comment

You can see the difference between the two strategies. In the first Robert wasn't given a chance to put across his position. He was simply blamed for what had gone wrong and told to put it right. This strategy may well lead to resentment and hostility. The second dialogue is much better. Here, Jack draws the information out of Robert by asking open questions, 'Can you tell me about it?', and then asks Robert for his own solution: 'What do you think we should do about it?'. The problem is presented, the solution is found, and appropriate action is planned.

Also, Jack used 'you' in the first dialogue. This isolates Robert from the company, suggests the problem is entirely his and that he alone has to find the solution. In the second dialogue 'you' becomes 'we', the problem becomes a company problem, and the company will work together with Robert to find the solution. The use of 'we' in this context is less likely to alienate the appraisee, and thus less likely to create resentment against the organisation.

as a single package, as usually happens in practice, rather than have two or three different appraisal interviews that upset the flow of everyday work and don't really achieve anything extra.

That doesn't mean that *all* the above have to be included in every regular performance review. *Each* appraisal interview should be carefully designed, and its purposes clearly laid out. Appraisals carried out between times largely concern particular job openings (promotion and transfer).

PROBLEM AREAS

Many managers feel that the handing out of rewards and punishments should be kept separate from the rest of the appraisal procedure, particularly when the appraisal may include criticisms by the appraisee of the organisation or of the supervisor. If rewards are assigned separately, so the argument goes, the appraisee can be more open with the appraiser, and develop a better sense of trust. If the appraisee thinks you are forming subjective judgements on the basis of these criticisms (for example as to whether or not a full bonus is deserved!), and that you have the power to withhold bonuses, then the right trust can be hard to establish and the appraisee will not state their viewpoints openly.

Fortunately this argument does not apply to well-designed appraisal systems. It is not cost-effective or necessary to separate these two elements, of assigning rewards and punishments and encouraging openness on the part of the appraisee.

● The problem is surmounted by awarding bonuses on the basis of objective measures of performance.

For example, if the appraisee functions at 10 per cent over the performance objectives previously set, or 10 per cent over the average performer in their group, then the full bonus is awarded. If the figures are 10 per cent below, the bonus is withheld. In this way the system is not susceptible to the whims of an appraiser who wanted to reduce a pay bonus simply because the appraisee criticised their supervisor in the appraisal interview.

Even the best appraisal systems are, like anything involving humans, open to abuse. For example the appraiser may try to set objectives that the appraisee believes are too high, or the data that were used in the appraisal interview were inaccurate or biased. A good appraisal system gets around this problem by having

grievance procedures and **arbitration** where appraisees can approach other authorities if they believe they have been treated unfairly.

POINTS FOR DISCUSSION

1. Look at the list of purposes for carrying out appraisals given above. Which ones are used in your organisation? Give reasons why the others aren't used.

2. List three benefits of appraisal for (a) your organisation, (b) yourself.

3. What kinds of data are used in your organisation for performance reviews? Is it objective or subjective?

3
Appraisal Skills Required

SUMMARY

The main points of this chapter are that:

- Both you and the appraisee should be trained in interviewing techniques, negotiation, understanding and interpreting the data and listening to the other person.

- You should be trained in job analysis, basic counselling skills and designing the appriasal interview.

- The appraisee should be trained to prepare for the interview and develop self-awareness.

An appraisal system cannot work properly without due regard to the training both you and the appraisee need in your respective roles. There are a range of skills both parties need to carry out the appraisal properly.

One problem that can arise is to get managers to admit to their weaknesses regarding the skills required. They may believe they have the requisite skills, such as interviewing and negotiation, when this is not the case. It is the responsibility of the organisation to ensure the appropriate skills are obtained.

One cannot separate the different skills required by individuals involved in appraisals; they are too closely linked. For instance, those listed below under the heading of 'negotiation' largely apply to general interviews. These skills are considered separately for the sake of clarity.

INTERVIEWING SKILLS

There are many kinds of interviewing situation and they require different kinds of skills. These include:

- selection interviewing (both one-to-one and panel)
- media interviewing
- appraisal interviewing
- counselling (which is a form of interviewing).

Here we focus on appraisal interviewing, though as discussed earlier, there are similarities with selection interviewing. Counselling interviewing will be discussed in more detail below as it is a subject in its own right.

Certain rules apply across all kinds of interviewing, including the appraisal interview. Interviewing is a **communication skill**. Before an effective interview can take place, both parties need to know what the other party expects. If both parties agree on the purpose of the interview, it is more likely to succeed. If not, then neither party will really listen to what the other has to say. Since they are expecting different things, they will hear different things. Suppose you are only interested in reviewing the performance of the appraisee and setting new objectives for the coming year, but the appraisee wishes to discuss training needs. You may find yourselves talking at cross-purposes and achieve little except mutual dissatisfaction. You will realise that the appraisee is dissatisfied, and the appraisee will be unhappy that their training needs haven't been met. This shows the need for each party to *listen* to what the other is saying.

Empathy

A good interviewer or interviewee will always try to appreciate the other person's point of view, to try and understand *why* they are saying what they are saying, as well as *what* they are saying. This leads to **empathy**, and an increased likelihood of mutual goodwill. It is then more probable that conclusions can be reached which are satisfactory to both parties. In the example above, if you listen to the appraisee's views on training, and act on them, the outcome of the appraisal is more likely to satisfy both parties.

The purposes of the interview

These may be:

- to establish training needs
- to assess past performance and assign rewards/punishments
- to set targets for future performance
- to determine suitability for promotion/transfer
- to assess future potential.

Within the general framework, each party may wish to raise specific points. For example, the appraisee may wish to complain about poor supervision. It is useful if the appraiser knows that this point will be raised in order to prepare an answer to it. This is rather like Question Time in the House of Commons, where the questioner presents the question well in advance, so that the minister has time to formulate a well-considered answer.

Finding background information

If you know the appraisee has a problem with supervision before the interview takes place, you can look into the possible reasons behind it. In the interview itself you are only going to hear the appraisee's side of the argument, and it would be extremely unwise to base any decisions on partial data. Before the interview takes place, go and see the appraisee's supervisor and get their view. The supervisor may not realise there is a problem, and a chat with the appraiser may itself solve it. Perhaps the supervisor is unaware of some personal circumstance of the appraisee that is affecting work performance, such as overtiredness due to a new baby. If the supervisor thought the poor performance was due to laziness then it is likely that this would cause trouble between supervisor and appraisee. In this case the solution is simple: the supervisor should be more sympathetic with the appraisee, and perhaps transfer some of their workload temporarily to ease the situation.

This example is an illustration of a lack of communication, the major cause of organisational inefficiency and employee dissatisfaction. The appraisal system is designed to increase communication.

In many cases the solution won't be this simple. For instance, if there is a personality clash between the supervisor and the appraisee, it may only be soluble by transferring one party (usually the employee). The important point is that it is *crucial* that you make an effort to understand both sides of any problem, before the appraisal interview.

Preparing for the interview

It should not be necessary to say that both parties need to be prepared for the appraisal interview, but in many real life cases one or both parties go into the interview not knowing what they are going to say, or how they are going to respond to what the other party is going to say. This guarantees an unsatisfactory outcome.

Both parties should be prepared

Once the purposes of the interview have been established, the way to obtain a better outcome is for *both parties* to work out what information they need to collect for the interview. They should prepare answers to questions the other party is posing, and prepare their own questions. More attention is paid to the collecting of information in the next chapter, because this is a key issue in appraisal. Relevant information should be collected and collated, and a copy of the **pre-appraisal report** given to both you and the appraisee before the interview. From this simple document both parties can prepare questions and discussion points.

Both parties in the appraisal need to be aware of the **structure** of the interview. The design of this will usually lie with you, as the one who first determined the purposes of the appraisal. You will now decide *what* should be discussed and *when*, ensuring a section of the interview is open for the appraisee to raise issues they consider important. Thus the structure of the interview is controlled by you. This does not harm the interests of the appraisee, as long as they are given a chance to raise the points they feel important. The structure of the appraisal interview will be considered in more depth later.

NEGOTIATING SKILLS

It is important for both you and the appraisee to have good negotiating skills. Negotiation is not a process whereby two parties start from different positions and reach a compromise that satisfies neither party.

* The aim of good negotiation is a **win-win situation** where, even if both parties start from a different stand-point, they can both feel they have benefited.

A sense of equality

One important prerequisite for good negotiation is a sense of **equality** between the two parties. You are likely to be of higher rank than the appraisee, and it may be difficult to achieve true equality. If the two parties need to negotiate away their differences, then the appraisee must not have to fear any recriminations for acting as your equal.

It is very difficult to attain true equality between individuals of different rank. Unconscious processes can come into play. Appraisees may not put forward propositions and ideas as strongly as they should, and are also more ready to accept ideas that you propose. The opposite may be true for you, as you may put forward ideas more forcefully, and be less likely to listen properly to the ideas of the appraisee. This illustrates the importance of both parties consciously behaving as equals. This will minimise the problem.

Eight rules for successful negotiation

There are certain **rules** that should be followed in order to negotiate successfully. Some of these may appear a little harsh, particularly when trying to design an appraisal interview that is open and fair, with both parties interacting on a friendly basis. Many of the rules of negotiation don't seem conducive to such behaviour, but remember that they are based on strategies used by skilled negotiators bargaining between organisations. They are not necessarily harsh; it depends on how and where they are used. The appraisal interview is very different from negotiating at an organisational level, but the same rules apply to both situations.

If both parties are aware of the rules, of the way each other is behaving, misunderstandings are less likely to occur.

The rules are:

1. Avoiding irritators
These include words and phrases that have little positive effect on the negotiation, but irritate the other side. This might include suggesting that your own position is 'fair' when it patently is not, or implies that the other party's position is not fair. This category also includes offensive and insulting statements, or statements based on incomplete information: for example, if you tell the appraisee that they are 'incompetent' because they haven't achieved certain targets, without looking into the reasons why the targets haven't been met.

2. Counter-proposals
This is where one side makes a suggestion, and the other side makes a counter-suggestion, totally ignoring the suggestion from the first side. This is an issue of listening. As mentioned elsewhere listening is important in any appraisal interview. If one party ignores the other by simply presenting its own position, it is not listening. For instance, the appraisee may say 'I have not achieved my productivity targets because the reports have not been reaching me on time.' The appraisee is suggesting that there is a communication problem within the organisation. Instead of agreeing to look into

the matter, you may simply suggest that the targets haven't been reached because the appraisee does not manage time effectively, and suggest a time management course. In other words you have not listened. This is not an effective way to run an appraisal interview.

3. Aggressive behaviour

This arises when the interview is allowed to get heated, where conflict and hostility become overt. The situation can quickly spiral and become out of control. This is unlikely to occur in many appraisal situations for a number of reasons. Even though a sense of equality may be present, the appraisee will probably be a little afraid of displaying too much equality, such as acting aggressively towards you. Likewise you may well feel that acting aggressively may be exploiting your own superior status in a way that is unacceptable You are also in a position to ensure disagreements do not become open conflict. Another reason why aggressive behaviour does not often occur is that both parties belong to the same organisation, and so probably know each other.

4. Argument dilution

This is a more subtle side of negotiation. It occurs when one side justifies a position by using too many supporting arguments. This is a self-defeating process. The more arguments one uses in support of a position, the more likely it is that the other party can effectively argue against that position, by turning one of these supporting arguments around. Once one argument collapses, the whole position may collapse.

For instance, the appraisee may argue that he needs a particular type of training, using a whole string of arguments to support this position, such as increased productivity, benefits outweighing costs, efficiency, increased knowledge base, and the future potential of the individual. The organisation may not be able to argue against most of these reasons, but may not believe the appraisee is likely to stay long enough to justify the increased outlay. So the final argument, future potential, is used by you to justify not expending resources on training the appraisee. Thus the appraisee, instead of providing a list of solid reasons why the training should be provided, has undermined his own position by presenting too many reasons.

5. Behaviour labelling

This is a technique used to keep the discussion rational, and to slow it down. It involves tagging statements with **prior indicators** that show what the individual is going to say. For instance, instead of saying, 'I would like a pay rise' the appraisee might say 'I'm going to ask you a question. I would like a pay rise.' This technique can be used when the discussion seems to be losing direction, or when issues are being covered too rapidly. Behaviour labelling enables either party to slow the discussion down or get it back on course. It is a simple but effective technique.

6. Testing understanding and summarising

This is used to ensure that the individual has understood what the other party is trying to say, and to give themselves time to think of a response. If you have made a proposal, and the appraisee wishes to make it clear in his head, it is useful if he repeats it in his own words and checks with you to ensure it is understood properly.

For example, if the discussion has centred on training needs, you should sum up by stating in simple terms the agreed training needs of the appraisee. For example, 'It seems then that you would benefit from a course on report writing, which should improve the quality of your writing and ensure reports reach your supervisor on time. Would you agree with that?'. If you have made an error, this will immediately become obvious when the appraisee responds, 'I do agree, but you have not mentioned my need for training in stress management that I mentioned earlier'.

7. Seeking information

Suppose the other party has put forward a proposal, but has not fully explained their position. The good negotiator will ask for the further information required. This is also a useful strategy for controlling the situation. A carefully directed question will steer the discussion in a particular direction. 'I know you are unhappy in the sales department, but you say you have a talent for marketing. Would you explain to me why you believe you would be more suited to the marketing department?'

8. Feelings commentary

This phrase describes the way individuals express their feelings. Effective negotiators are more likely to express the way they feel than ineffective negotiators. In the case of appraisal interviews, if you express your feelings—and are perhaps openly critical of some aspect of the organisation—you are more likely to obtain the trust of the appraisee. It shows you are willing to let your guard down, to 'expose your throat', and the appraisee is then more likely to state their position more openly. This of course is also an important aspect of counselling.

Understanding the data

In the next chapter, various forms of data are described that can be used in the appraisal interview. Some of these are fairly complex, and so both parties may need training in order to understand them. For instance, if a personality questionnaire is given to the appraisee, to understand the results both you and the appraisee need to appreciate the definitions of the traits that are used, and the explanations for the results put forward by the psychologist. If supervisor ratings are used, it is important that both parties interpret each rating in the same way otherwise understanding, and hence communication, will be adversely affected. If one question reads, 'Rate the appraisee on overall performance', apart from being a badly worded question which the supervisor probably won't understand, it may be interpreted in different ways by the two parties.

Active listening skills

It is important for both parties to engage in **active listening**. This is crucial for a good appraisal interview. They should show each other that they are being listened to properly, not simply heard, by concentrating on what is being said and not losing interest. The basic rules are:

- don't make hasty judgements
- don't listen selectively
- don't interrupt
- feed back the information to ensure it has been heard properly.

The appraiser who makes hasty judgements without hearing all sides of an argument is ineffective. If you don't listen to all the appraisee has to say then you may miss something of value. Likewise for the appraiser who listens selectively. If you have decided before the appraisal interview what your conclusions will be, and only hear what you want to hear, then why have the appraisal at all?

Apart from being simple rudeness, constant interruptions can upset the flow of the appraisee's comments. Interruptions are justified when the appraisee (or the appraiser for that matter) is rambling, or when one party doesn't understand what the other is saying, but not otherwise. If something comes to mind, then instead of interrupting, make a note of it, to enable you to remember what to say once the speaker has finished.

APPRAISER SKILLS

You may well need training in job analysis, interviewing techniques as an interviewer, basic counselling skills, and on how to design appraisal interviews. There are also a number of other skills required that are harder to categorise, but are listed below.

Job analysis

A key element of appraisal interviewing is the job analysis. If there is no adequate job description available this analysis may need to be carried out before the appraisal. This is described in more detail in Chapter 5. It will suffice to state here that by analysing the job of the appraisee you learn about that job in very great detail. You become aware of:

- how the job is carried out
- the objectives that are reasonable to set someone performing the job
- the limitations on performance imposed by the job
- how the job might need to be changed
- the role of the job within the organisation.

You won't always have to go through the whole process of job analysis and job description. In more efficient companies, up-to-date and complete job descriptions will be on hand, but the good appraiser should not always rely on this information being available. There is no point in using a job description that is out of date (and they can become out of date very quickly). The information may be wrong. The best way to find out whether a job description is out of date is to *ask the person* performing the job, and perhaps their supervisor.

Interviewer skills

Interviewing involves more than an informal chat between two people, or a set of questions chosen simply because they 'sound good'. Accurate conclusions cannot be drawn from this kind of situation. A good interview needs to fulfil certain requirements, including:

- the right location
- creating a relaxed atmosphere
- asking the right questions
- structuring the interview (are the questions predetermined or do they arise from the interview itself?)
- personal skills
- recording the data accurately.

These requirements will ensure that as much useful information is extracted as possible.

You need to learn the right interviewing skills for standard appraisal purposes, and also for staff selection purposes.

Question-formatting

Certain interviewing skills are specific to the role of appraiser. **Formatting the questions** themselves is an important one. Questions should normally be open-ended, that is, force the appraisee to answer in greater detail than in a simple yes/no fashion. For example, 'why do you think your performance has been below standard recently?' is better than 'Has your performance been below standard recently?'. The former leads to a better two-way discussion. You can respond to the appraisee's answers with further questions to explore the information obtained; ideas expressed can be linked together better, and clarity will be ensured. It is inefficient to go on asking closed questions, and leading questions such as 'Your performance has been poor because your husband left you, hasn't it?', though closed questions can be useful for gathering basic information.

Counselling skills you will need

It is important for you to have counselling skills, though you should never try to take the place of the professional counsellor. There are plenty of experts, should that be necessary. The reason for you having training in basic counselling skills is that these skills are likely to be needed at unpredictable times. For instance, when the appraisee is discussing the reasons for poor recent performance, they may blurt out that their partner is about to leave them. This situation calls for a little tact and diplomacy on your part.

You basically need to be gentle, to display empathy with the appraisee, and display good listening skills. Counselling is not a matter of telling someone what to do. It is essential for the individual to make his or her own decisions. The most that the counsellor can do is to offer advice.

Counselling skills are also important in the redundancy appraisal. If the appraisee knows the potential consequences of a poor performance, it can be quite traumatic. The situation is equally serious in the vocational assessment appraisal, in cases where the appraisee knows they have been sacked, and may be experiencing personal problems originating from that fact.

Designing the appraisal interview

One key skill you will need is that of designing the interview itself. It is essential that the interview is well-structured. This isn't just a matter of ensuring you collect the right information in the interview, though clearly this is the desired aim. In order to achieve this aim you should carefully consider the purposes of the interview, the collection of preliminary data, and the form of the interview itself.

Other important appraiser skills

Effective use of data
You need the ability to use available data effectively, to consider various options, and to put these options to the appraisee in a reasonable fashion. This involves a great deal of skill and tact. You could simply set high targets and tell the appraisee to achieve them. It is more difficult, but more effective, to *sell* the options to the appraisee, to show them how the objectives are reasonable. This in turn will lead the appraisee to internalise the objectives, to accept them more fully, and be more willing to act on them.

Thus the appraiser's role is partly one of selling, but selling ideas rather than goods or services.

Constructive criticism
You should be able to criticise in a constructive fashion. It is easy to criticise someone's less than perfect work, but it is harder to criticise without isolating the appraisee and losing their trust. Don't spend the whole appraisal interview tearing apart the appraisee's work. That is not constructive. Apart from disillusioning the victim it is also a waste of time. If there is a need to criticise then do so in a reasonable fashion, and follow up with constructive suggestions as to how to improve things. For instance, if a manager is always rushing around trying to organise things without seeming to get anything done, it is right that they should be criticised. But if this is followed up by the constructive proposal that they should

attend a time management course, then the criticism becomes productive.

A firm manner

You do need a certain firmness of manner, which should be used at appropriate times. It is for you to keep the appraisal interview on course, to keep to the structure of the interview and not allow serious diversions. If the interview is going astray, you should bring it back to the subject in question. Firmness of manner means assertiveness, not aggression. It means ensuring you keep control of the situation, always politely, but always with authority.

Discretion

It is essential that you are discreet. The appraisee must be able to trust you to keep whatever is discussed confidential. The appraisee will be more open if you have promised that anything that is said will not be disclosed to others.

Objective judgements

You should be able to make objective judgements based on accurate data in an unbiased fashion. This is not necessarily easy, especially when you are the appraisee's supervisor and there is antagonism between. you. If there is bad feeling, it may be best if the supervisor is not the appraiser (see Chapter 4).

Supervisor ratings

Another skill you will require, and one often not given due consideration, is the ability to design and use supervisor rating forms. This involves:

- designing supervisor rating questionnaires that are appropriate to particular circumstances
- training supervisors etc to fill them in correctly
- interpreting them accurately.

Supervisor ratings (Chapter 6) are often used as performance indicators. Use them with great caution as ratings are necessarily subjective judgements.

APPRAISEE SKILLS

The skills required by the appraisee were largely covered earlier, but there are a few points to make. The appraisee is the interviewee, and like any interviewee wants to come out of the appraisal 'looking good'. In order for this to happen they must:

- be prepared
- put themselves across well

The appraisee is in a different role to the selection interviewee, as they usually know you, and 'first impressions' will not be a relevant consideration.

Preparing for the appraisal

Appraisees should assess their performance over the period under consideration. It is important for them to relate performance to previously set objectives, so that when you ask questions useful answers can be provided. It is also important to try to ensure that as many as possible of your questions are anticipated, and answers prepared.

Preparation should also be made regarding the future. What sort of objectives ought to be set? What training is needed? In what direction is the appraisee's career going? Is the level of responsibility adequate? How should performance be improved? Treat the appraisal as a career evaluation. The appraisal interview is a chance to try and change things that are wrong, to improve one's conditions and circumstances, and create opportunities for career development.

Developing self-awareness

The appraisee should analyse his own strengths and weaknesses before the interview. This skill is called developing self-awareness, and involves the ability to congratulate or criticise oneself appropriately. It is harder to acquire than might be imagined. The appraisee has to consider the areas where he was particularly successful or unsuccessful, and look into the reasons why.

Case study: Listening skills

Philippa Harvey was regional sales manager in the South West for Proctor's, a large firm of paper manufacturers. A few months previously she had been very happy, she was very good at her job and everyone knew it. Her region consistently outperformed other regions, and this was in large part due to her personal efforts. Then she had been told unofficially by her friend, Rachel Jones at Head Office, that the vacancy for the post of national sales director was going to become vacant soon, and that she was by far the best candidate—if she was interested. She was very interested, and when the post had been publicised she had applied immediately.

That was when things began to go wrong. When she heard nothing for a few weeks, she telephoned Rachel to find out what was happening. Rachel was very evasive, and said that the directors hadn't considered the applications yet. So Philippa waited another couple of weeks. Finally, she received a letter which said that unfortunately she had not got the post, but thank you for applying.

Philippa was livid. She repeatedly phoned Head Office for an explanation but got nowhere. She felt rejected by the organisation, and this showed in her work, which deteriorated quite considerably. After a couple of months, during which time she was far from happy, she was called to Head Office for appraisal. The appraiser was Ashley Edwards, one of the directors.

The interview was very heated. Ashley knew that Philippa had been turned down for the head office post in favour of someone from outside the organisation who was very experienced at this level. What he wasn't prepared for was the level of Philippa's anger. When he told Philippa why she hadn't got the post she just managed to control her temper and explained that she felt the company had let her down very badly, that after so many years' experience they had not even interviewed her for the post—though she was supposedly the best candidate—and they had not discussed with her the reasons why she hadn't got the post. Anyway, who was this person who had got the job? As the company was only interested in talking to her now when they saw weaknesses in her performance it was obvious they still didn't care about her needs. At that point she resigned.

Comment
Philippa's case is rather unfortunate. She was obviously very valuable to the company; she had attained the status of regional sales manager and was performing very well. They didn't want to lose her. When the national vacancy arose it is unfortunate that they didn't even interview her, to show they appreciated her talents enough to consider her for the post. The breaking point came when her rejection simply consisted of a short non-explanatory letter. Instead of this letter Philippa should have been told face to face that she hadn't been given the post, and the reasons for the decision explained (ie a kind of appraisal). It is important for organisations in this situation to show they value the individual. Proctor's did not do this and so they lost a good worker.

POINTS FOR DISCUSSION

1. Think about the training you have had for carrying out appraisals. Does it cover all aspects of the appraisals you carry out? In what areas do you need further taining?

2. A member of your tcam is due for a performance review. What are the main issues that should be addressed when preparing for the interview?

3. How should you train someone in negotiating skills?

4
The Role of Appraiser

SUMMARY

In this chapter we'll see how:

- There are various possibilities for who takes on the role of appraiser: line manager, supervisor, employer, personnel manager/officer, specially trained appraisal officer.

- There are arguments for and against each of these being the appraiser. The final choice will depend on the organisation and the individual being appraised.

Preparation is *crucial* to the success of any appraisal. Both you and the appraisee need to put a lot of time and effort into preparing for the appraisal, or it will not succeed.

Several decisions have to be made before preparations can begin for the appraisal interview. You, representing the organisation, usually decide:

- when the appraisal will occur
- what its purposes are
- the data that need to be collected
- the structure of the interview.

This chapter, and the two following, consider the decisions being made when preparing for the appraisal. These include:

- who should be the appraiser
- the purposes of the appraisal
- the type and extent of data to be collected
- how the data should be collected

- preparing the pre-appraisal report
- ensuring the appraisee has seen and understood the report
- determining discussion points arising from the report and any other sources
- ensuring each party understands what the other wants to achieve
- planning the appraisal interview itself.

WHO SHOULD DO THE APPRAISING?

There are various candidates for the role of appraiser. They include:

- the line manager
- the appraisee's immediate supervisor
- the employer
- the personnel manager
- a specially trained appraisal officer whose major function is to carry out staff appraisals.

There are valid arguments for all these individuals to be the appraiser, and equally valid arguments why none of them are ideal in all circumstances. The choice of appraiser will depend on such factors as availability, type of appraisal, rank of the person being appraised, and size of organisation. Small organisations may not have individuals who fill all the roles above. Few organisations, even large ones, have anyone whose major function is to carry out appraisals, as in the past the role of appraiser has been part of the function of the line manager.

What are the arguments for and against each of these?

The immediate supervisor or line manager
This is not usually the best person to act as appraiser, though in most organisations they do. Admittedly there are good reasons *for* the appraisal being carried out by such a person. Others may know too little about the appraisee's work, or the general work of the department, particularly if it is very specialist, such as a design department. They may be unable to assess previous performance accurately or to provide reasonable objectives. These problems can usually be surmounted by an appraiser with some knowledge of what the appraisee does, by carrying out detailed research into the

job before the interview, and ensuring adequate data is available about both the job and the person.

Another argument for having the appraisal with the supervisor or manager is that it may be seen as betrayal if anyone else is used. This is not a valid argument. If company policy is to have someone other than the supervisor carry out the appraisal, then the supervisor is unlikely to question it.

● The best argument *against* the supervisor or line manager carrying out the appraisal is their close working relationship. This may make it difficult for either or both parties to express themselves fully, especially if the appraisee wishes to criticise the standard of supervision. The appraiser and appraisee have to work together on a daily basis, so any antagonism between them might reduce productivity and job satisfaction for both.

Sometimes, an appraisee's poor performance may be caused by difficulties in their relationship with their supervisor. For example what if the supervisor doesn't respect the abilities of the appraisee, or is always criticising their work? When the appraisee is questioned about his poor performance his answer is unlikely to be honest or complete. How do you tell someone you are not working very well because you don't like the way they treat you? This appraisal is likely to end without the two individuals getting to the root of the problem, which will then persist and may indeed worsen.

This example underlines the need for the appraisee to be able to talk to someone freely, to someone distanced from the situation, about whatever problems they feel exist. It is easier for the appraisee to discuss relationship problems at work if the appraiser is not someone they are involved with day-to-day.

There is another problem with using the supervisor or line manager. To do appraisals effectively, much appraiser training needs to be carried out, as we saw in the previous chapter. If the organisation has to train all its supervisors and line managers to do this costs may become unrealistically high. Far better to train a small group of individuals very well than many individuals poorly.

Using the employer

The best argument *for* the employer carrying out the appraisals is that he will, by assessing the performance of all employees, learn a great deal about how the company functions. A cynic might claim that this is also the best argument *against* the employer carrying out the appraisals!

In reality, the employer may be the best person to carry out appraisals in very small firms, but the time factor is clearly going to militate against this in bigger firms. Appraising staff takes time. An essential component of smooth operation it may be, but the employer has many roles to fulfil. Appraising staff is not likely to make the most efficient use of time.

The use of the employer as appraiser may also involve too large a difference between the rank of appraiser and appraisee. It may be difficult to establish a sense of equality at the appraisal interview. There is also the problem that the employer may not know enough about particular jobs and their requirements.

One apparent advantage of using employers (or other senior staff) as appraisers is that they are more likely to be aware of the corporate philosophy and objectives than someone of lower rank, and so should be in a good position to ensure that individual objectives link in with it. Unfortunately the real world does not function like this. It is often hard for someone at senior level to express corporate objectives in terms of practical individual objectives. In any case, where this is a consideration the organisation will be too large for the employer to carry out the appraisals.

Using the personnel manager
The personnel manager's job is to ensure that the human resources of the organisation are functioning properly. This may mean anything from employing the right numbers of people in the right jobs to making sure pay packets are filled correctly at the end of the week. Appraisal interviewing clearly falls within the role of the personnel manager and this is the best argument that he should carry out the interviews. He should be conversant with the appraisal system, with the jobs, and with the people doing the jobs. In medium sized firms the personnel manager may be able to carry out some appraisals. In larger firms, the personnel manager has overall responsibility for the appraisal system, but the appraisals themselves should be done by other members of the personnel department.

Using the specially trained appraisal officer
In larger organisations appraisals should be carried out by in-house specialists. There are a number of reasons for this:

● A specialist appraiser will have detailed knowledge about the jobs carried out within the organisation (by reading job descriptions, interviewing employees, etc).

● A specialist will appreciate the philosophy and objectives of the organisation, yet be able to interpret these in terms of individual employee needs.

● A specialist will be trained in the various skills required for effective appraisals.

● A specialist will be able to analyse the results of appraisals across the organisation and advise what targets to set, which departments are performing best, where problems lie, etc.

● Finally, perhaps most importantly, the judgements a specialist appraiser makes will apply in a similar fashion *across the organisation*.

On this last point, if the appraiser assesses individuals across the whole organisation, they will be able to make objective, comparable, and thus fair judgements between employees. Consistency between individuals is particularly important, especially when the purpose of the appraisal is promotion, transfer, redundancy, reward/punishment or determining training needs.

So who should be the appraiser?
There can be no single answer to this question. It depends mainly on:

● the size of the organisation
● the purposes of the appraisal

Generally speaking, though:

● If the organisation is very small (ie, where the employer has not separated the role of personnel from other functions), the employer is the right person to carry out the appraisal;
● in medium sized firms the personnel manager is the most appropriate appraiser;
● in larger firms the specialist appraiser in the personnel department will be able to carry out most appraisals most efficiently.

The line manager or supervisor is *not* appropriate if it is likely to damage the personal relationship between appraiser and appraisee after the interview, or if the appraisee is not going to speak out for fear of the consequences.

The use of line managers and supervisors as appraisers depends largely on the personality of the individuals and their day-to-day relationships with the employees. Organisations need to base their decisions on a systematic analysis of their own circumstances, resources and needs.

If the appraisal is for promotion/transfer or selection, it would be appropriate for the appraiser to be a manager from the department having the vacancy rather than a specialist from the personnel department. The organisation is examining the candidates for a vacancy and trying to place the right individual in it. The manager from the appropriate department will usually be more aware of the needs of that department than someone outside.

If the appraisee is a specialist, such as a research scientist, it may be inappropriate for an appraiser to come from outside the department. It would be unreasonable to expect that appraiser to know enough about the work of the scientist. After all, the training of a scientist takes many years and it would not be possible to condense it all into a short job description! In such cases the appraiser needs to be someone from the same department, with similar specialist knowledge. But even here care is needed. The appraisal may, if not carefully prepared, become too cosy, with the needs of the organisation coming second to the needs of the scientists within the department.

- This illustrates the need to be conscious at all times of the purposes of the appraisal in terms of the needs of the *organisation* as well as the individual and the department.

KEEPING THE OBJECTIVES IN VIEW

The purposes of appraisal were discussed in detail in Chapter 2. In summary, they are:

- regular performance review
- setting objectives
- assigning rewards/punishments
- determining training needs
- promotion/transfer
- selection
- redundancy

Case study: Who should be the appraiser?

Graham is a manager at Cloggs Shoes, a footwear manufacturer. He supervises the sales staff. He is also responsible for appraising the sales staff. Graham is very unpopular because of his rather authoritarian approach. He supervises by ordering people to do things, never considering the viewpoint of his subordinates. If the task is done well he rarely praises, if it is done badly he frequently criticises.

All sales staff have an annual performance review, along with more frequent meetings to discuss particular issues that arise. Jacqueline was very nervous about her appraisal interview. She did not like Graham, and on top of that, she had problems at home that were affecting her performance at work. Her poor performance was regularly criticised by Graham, who had little sympathy for personal problems. He strictly separated home life from work life, and expected everyone else to do the same. This criticism affected Jacqueline's performance even more.

When the interview started, Graham got straight to the point: 'Your performance has been deteriorating for the last six months, and it can't go on. You have to do something about it or you're out.' Jacqueline really needed to discuss why her performance was suffering, but she couldn't talk to Graham. She had little to say in response to Graham's charge, and the interview ended with even more hostility and dislike than there had been before it. After the interview Jacqueline went straight to see Graham's superior, to discuss what had happened and to find some way to sort out her problems, one of which was now her supervisor.

Comment
Jacqueline should have been appraised by someone other than her supervisor because part of her problem became the supervisor. Though the main problem was her personal difficulties, these were exacerbated by Graham. She needed to talk to someone who would be sympathetic, both about her personal difficulties and the quality of her supervision. If her supervisor had been more empathetic regarding her personal difficulties then maybe they wouldn't have affected her work performance.

Situations like these, where the employee is forced to 'go behind the supervisor's back' to a third person, can lead to further problems, ones that wouldn't have arisen had the original appraisal been carried out by someone other than Graham.

- vocational guidance
- assessing future potential
- job redesign

As noted earlier, these objectives are not mutually exclusive; several may be covered in the same interview.

It is crucial that the purposes of the appraisal are determined and understood right from the start. If you don't know exactly why the appraisal is being carried out, how can you possibly begin to organise it? If the appraisee doesn't know why he is being appraised, how can he formulate arguments and discussion points?

By being aware of why the appraisal is being carried out you will know what to include in it. If it is for a regular performance review, it will probably include setting future objectives and assigning rewards or punishments. Other elements will be included as and when required. The appraisee may wish to include purposes such as determining training needs. If the appraisee has just finished a probationary period, the appraisal will probably include an assessment of future potential. Appraisals for promotion/transfer and selection arise out of organisational need.

Apart from the regular performance review (which should be standardised across employees), appraisals arise out of **need**, either the need of the organisation or the need of the individual employee.

For details of these types of appraisal, see Chapter 2.

POINTS FOR DISCUSSION

1. Who in your own organisation is most likely to carry out appraisals? List reasons why this is (a) a good idea, (b) a bad idea.

2. Think of the members of your own team. What is the optimum time (or year, month, week, day) for them to have their regular performance review? What are your reasons for this?

3. Are there cases in your own organisation where a specially trained appraisal officer would be (a) more effective, (b) less effective, than a line manager for carrying out appraisals?

5
Job Description and Person Specification

SUMMARY

In this chapter about the next stage of preparation, we will see that:

- Different types of data are needed.

- The decision as to which data to use depends on the purposes of the appraisal.

- Data should be as objective and unbiased as possible.

- The job description should be up-to-date and complete.

- The person specification is derived from the job description and tells us about the type of individual who should be employed on the job.

WHAT DATA ARE NEEDED?

Several types of data are relevant to appraisal interviews. You need to decide which are necessary *after* you have determined the purposes of the appraisal. Data should not be collected for the sake of it. There is little point in using psychometric test results for a simple performance review. Similarly, all data that is relevant should be collected. If you haven't obtained supervisor ratings and comments, and the appraisee suggests that they are not getting along well with their colleagues, you will not be able to form a balanced judgement about why these problems exist. The appraisee may suggest that the problem lies with colleagues. but the supervisor may suggest that the problem lies with the appraisee. You need both sides of the argument.

Whichever data are used, try to ensure they are as **objective** and **unbiased** as possible. This is impossible to achieve totally, as individuals have to make subjective judgements and decisions. But be aware when you are making subjective judgements, and appreciate why errors of judgement may arise.

The major types of data used in appraisals are:

- job description
- person specification
- performance criteria
- previous objectives
- psychometric testing

The first two relate specifically to the needs of the job, and are considered in this chapter. The others relate to the individual appraisee, or the interaction between the appraisee and the job, and are considered in the next chapter.

JOB DESCRIPTION

This is an essential type of information, particularly where you are not fully conversant with the job. As mentioned earlier, the job description should be *up-to-date* and *complete*, otherwise you will not be certain of the nature of the appraisee's job. In efficient organisations up-to-date job descriptions are available, but unfortunately this is not often the case. If there isn't one, you will have to devise one. The more you know about the appraisee's job in the first place, the easier it is to devise a job description.

The process of formulating a job description can be very time consuming, and you may need help to do it. If the appraisal system is going to succeed, the help of the personnel department in ensuring job descriptions are up-to-date is essential. A specialist appraiser won't have the time to devise these job descriptions.

What follows is a simple method of devising a job description. The description should be revised regularly using the same process. Jobs can change in character over quite short periods of time, partly due to the individuals involved in the job, who share tasks, transfer tasks, etc, and partly due to the organisation which may change the tasks involved. Many of these changes are peripheral, but it is important to incorporate them in the up-to-date job description. They may for example affect the personality requirements of the person carrying out the job (and hence the person specification for it).

Devising the job description

The first step is to carry out a **task analysis**. Basically this involves analysing the job to identify:

● what tasks are done
● how long they take
● how often they are carried out.

There are various ways of obtaining this information:

● Check whether an out-of-date job description exists. If there isn't a detailed one there may be a summary that has been used for advertising purposes.

● Observe the job being done.

● Ask the appraisee to keep a diary of the tasks carried out over a particular period of time, perhaps a few weeks. You can then analyse these tasks in terms of frequency, time taken, etc.

● Interview the appraisee to see whether any preliminary conclusions you have drawn are valid. The appraisee is a useful source of information about the work. Other tasks the appraisee does may not have been included, in which case these and others can be discussed in more detail.

● Interview others doing the same job.

● Interview the supervisor.

● The personnel department may be able to help reveal aspects of the job that are neglected, ie not carried out by the appraisee.

In order to identify the key elements of the job, where the appraisee's abilities are being put to the best use, ask the supervisor to record **critical incidents**. He or she is asked to recall incidents that showed someone doing the job in an excellent manner, and others that showed them doing it badly. These incidents will show which elements of the job are crucial and also help devise the person specification, described in the next section.

On the right is a sample form for the **task analysis**, followed by explanatory notes for filling it in.

TASK ANALYSIS

Job title: Department:

Company: Date:

Appraisee's name:

Supervisor's name:

Appraiser's name:

Task	Knowledge/Skills	Aptitudes	Personality
1.			
2.			
3.			
4.			
5.			
6.			
7.			
8.			
9.			
10.			

Fig. 1   Sample form for task analysis

Task analysis: explanatory notes

This checklist is used in conjunction with the job description and person specification. It enables the appraiser to analyse the tasks carried out by the appraisee, and the knowledge/ skills, aptitude and personality characteristics required. It is often useful to obtain help filling it in from the people doing the job and the supervisor.

The task analysis is used for designing the job description and person specification. The questionnaire above is arranged in four columns: task, knowledge/skills, aptitudes, and attitude.

Task

The individual tasks carried out by the appraisee are entered here. If possible, include a percentage figure for each task showing the amount of time spent on it. If this is not done, it may mistakenly be assumed that the employee spends the same time on each task, and the job description may be misleading if this isn't really so.

Knowledge/skills

What knowledge and/or skills are required for the task? For instance, educational qualifications, knowledge of a geographical area, and skills obtained at work, etc.

Aptitudes

What general abilities are required for the task? For instance, mechanical aptitude, numerical aptitude, verbal reasoning.

Personality

What personality characteristics are required of the appraisee to do the job well? For instance, patience, extroversion, competitiveness.

Make sure that the task analysis is carried out carefully. Very often a job hasn't previously been analysed in any depth, so the exercise may take a little time, but it will be worthwhile.

Putting the job description together

The information that you have built up using the task analysis can be put together into a job description. The job description contains five areas:

1. *Purpose of the job*: sets out the organisational objectives of the appointment.

2. *Position in the organisation*: shows to whom the individual should report, his or her department, perhaps including an organisational chart.

JOB DESCRIPTION

Job Title: Department:

Company: Date:

Prepared by: Position:

Job title:
Department:
Responsible to:
Responsible for:
Number employed on this work:
Position from which candidates for this job might come:
Avenues of promotion/transfer from this position:

Purpose/objects of work:

Main duties/activities:

Forms/equipment:

Contacts:

Discretion:

Checking:

Supervision required:

Supervision given:

Other responsibilities:

Working conditions/conditions of service:

Personal requirements:

Other information:

Please continue on a separate sheet if necessary.

Fig. 2   Example of a job description form

3. *Principal duties and responsibilities*: lists the key tasks the individual will perform. It also indicates level of authority.

4. *Specific tasks*: sets out in more detail what particular tasks have to be done and how they are carried out.

5. *Working relationships*: refers to those with whom the individual has contact, whether superiors, subordinates, colleagues, or people outside the organisation such as customers, salespeople.

The job description also includes information about the personal factors required of an individual doing the job and the education and training needed.

The job description is used in the appraisal interview as the major yardstick against which to assess performance. A job description is needed for all types of appraisal. An example of a job description form is given on page 67.

Job description—explanatory notes

It is crucial to understand the nature and purposes of the job. In order to define the job, the tasks involved, and the personal characteristics required of the appraisee, the job description is used.

The following notes will help you complete a job description. Make sure the form is filled in accurately, and in detail.

Purposes/objects of work
A summary of why the job exists, or is being created.

Main duties/activities
A list of the main tasks involved in the job, with some indication of the time spent on each. This information can be derived from the task analysis. Where does the work come from and where does it go to?

Forms/equipment
Does the appraisee need to complete or maintain any forms or records? Give examples. Do they need to use any machines or equipment? Illustrate.

Contacts
Indicate the extent, frequency and nature of any contact with other employees, organisations, or members of the public.

Discretion
Does the work entail following written (eg manual) or oral (eg supervisor) instructions? How far can the appraisee vary the methods of work or the order in which tasks are done?

Checking
Who checks the appraisee's work, how often, and by what method?

Supervision required
On that matters and how often does the appraisee receive instruction from superiors? What matters need to be referred to a superior for approval, or to be dealt with, and how often?

Supervision given
What authority does the appraisee have as to: assigning work, checking work, discipline, dealing with grievances, recommending appointments, salary increases, transfers, promotion, discharges and performance assessment?

Other responsibilities
Use this section for any other responsibilities of the appraisee that haven't been covered in other sections.

Working conditions/conditions of service
What are the conditions/environment under which work is carried out? What facilities are provided? How long does it take to learn the job? What are the rates of pay? Is it an hourly rate or commission-based?

Personal requirements
Education, skills, knowledge, personality.

Other information
This section can be used to include any information thought relevant to the job description that is not contained in any other section.

If a job description is already available, with less information than given here, it may well suffice. But do ensure that your own job description covers all the points raised above.

PERSON SPECIFICATION

The person specification describes the individual abilities and characteristics needed for the job, based on the job description. They are ones:

- essential for good performance
- desirable for good performance
- conflicting with good performance, ie if the person has this particular characteristic then it is likely that they will perform more poorly in the job because of it.

Six main headings

The person specification includes different sorts of information about the individual, categorised into six points. The information obtained on each point *must* be relevant to the job. Irrelevant information is not included, as it may bias any findings or conclusions. In many cases not all points are necessary. The six points are:

1. *Qualifications:* educational background, including vocational training and qualifications.

2. *Intelligence/aptitudes:* the level of general ability, perhaps measured by IQ, numerical or verbal ability, manual dexterity, etc.

3. *Personality:* is the individual who is good at the job likely to be extroverted, emotionally stable, dominant, aggressive?

4. *Interests:* how might the individual spend their free time? What might they want to do in the future? Are these interests primarily intellectual, artistic, social, practical, entrepreneurial?

5. *Motivation:* will the individual be motivated by money, status, praise?

6. *Appearance/circumstances:* this might include information on sex, age, height, build, tidiness of dress, speech. It also includes family factors, such as availability for travel or moving from area to area. For many jobs a lot of this information would be irrelevant and if so should *not* be included.

PERSON SPECIFICATION

Job Title: Department:

Company: Dates:

Prepared by: Position:

	Essential	*Desirable*	*Conflicting*
1. Qualifications			
2. Intelligence/ aptitudes			
3. Personality			
4. Interests			
5. Motivation			
6. Appearance/ circumstances			

Fig. 3   Example of a person specification form

Person specification—explanatory notes
The person specification comprises a list of characteristics sought in the ideal applicant for a job. It is based on inferences made from the job description about the personal qualities required.

The checklist will help ensure all the key qualities are included. Its framework is as follows:

Qualifications
Education, vocational qualifications, experience.

Intelligence/aptitudes
General intellectual capacity. Specific aptitudes, eg manual dexterity, verbal ability, numerical ability.

Personality
Personal characteristics required both in order to do the job effectively and to work well with colleagues.

Interests
Intellectual, practical, social, artistic.

Motivation
Money, status, personal esteem, friends.

Appearance/circumstances
Personal, family factors (eg locality, hours worked).

The information for the person specification is placed under one of the three headings:

- essential: the qualities placed under this heading are considered essential for the proper performance of the job. It is important not to have too many essential qualities or it may be impossible to find anyone who meets the specifications!

- desirable: qualities that would be useful in the applicant, but not essential.

- conflicting: a very useful category as it is often important to indicate characteristics that would make applicants positively unsuitable.

When using the checklist, the appraiser should try to include at least one characteristic under each heading (ie a minimum of six, rather than 18, characteristics), as this will help describe the 'ideal person' more accurately, though it is not always possible.

It is useful when devising the person specification to use a checklist like the one shown below. You can then, using the job description already designed, and perhaps with help from the appraisee's supervisor, fill in the checklist.

Examples
Examples of the use of the six points might include:

- *Qualifications:* a teacher would need an appropriate degree. A bricklayer would need to be time-served. Sales staff may not need particular qualifications, but a general education to GCSE or A level standard.

- *Intelligence/aptitude:* a component assembler in a factory would need manual dexterity. A bank manager would need a reasonable amount of general intelligence and a facility for numbers.

- *Personality:* a salesperson might need to be extroverted, and perhaps insensitive (so they are not affected by rebuttals). A self-employed person needs self-discipline. A diver needs courage.

- *Interests:* a scientist would need to be interested in analysing new ideas. An engineer needs to be interested in mechanical devices.

- *Motivation:* a salesperson is likely to be motivated by the amount of commission that can be earned rather than the quality of the product. A gardener may be more motivated by the results of his work than money.

- *Appearance/circumstances:* a store manager has to dress appropriately in a suit. A lorry driver's family needs to accept that he will stay away overnight perhaps once or twice a week.

The completed person specification is a real help when analysing the performance of the appraisee. The appraiser matches the qualities of the appraisee as judged from curriculum vitae, psychometric tests, performance, etc to the person specification, and concentrates on those areas where there is an apparent mismatch. A mismatch *does not* mean that the person is unsuited to the post. It could be rectified by training, or you may find on discussing the issue with the appraisee that the person specification wasn't accurate or complete, and that a different characteristic was just as appropriate. This is particularly true for personality charactistics, where people with widely disparate attributes do equally well at the same job.

Case study: Devising the job description

Charles has just been given responsibility for all marketing personnel. Part of his work involves appraising everyone in the department. Wanting to be thorough, Charles wishes to update the relevant job descriptions before carrying out any appraisals. Unfortunately, his superiors don't see things the same way. If Charles is going to update all the relevant job descriptions properly then he will need to spend a large amount of time on the task, and enlist the help of others. Unfortunately the company does not like the idea of Charles spending some weeks revising and updating the job descriptions.

This leaves Charles responsible for something he cannot carry out to the best of his ability. Charles must use the information he has (short job descriptions made up for advertising purposes) for carrying out the appraisals.

Charles devises a questionnaire that can be sent to all employees. The questionnaire brings together information on task analysis, job description and person specification. Because people are often loath to fill in forms, Charles partially completes them using the information he has. Then, when an appraisal is due, he asks the appraisee to complete the questionnaire, to indicate whether the information is correct, and what should be added and what taken away.

Comment
Using this method Charles has obtained a fairly clear idea of the different jobs in the marketing department without taking up too much company time, and without upsetting employees with a long-winded, time-consuming questionnaire. He can now carry out more effective appraisals.

A key management tool

The person specification is a key part of most appraisals, even regular performance reviews, where performance is being assessed and future targets set. This is because:

- it will help determine why an appraisee has failed to reach particular targets;
- it will help both parties get to the root of the problem more quickly;
- it is useful when assessing the appraisee's training requirements with regard to the job.

An example of a person specification form and explanatory notes are given on page 72.

POINTS FOR DISCUSSION

1. Carry out a task analysis of your own job. What can you learn from this?

2. Write out your own job description and person specification in a form suitable for use in an appraisal.

3. How can subjective data be made more objective?

6
How to Collect the Right Data

SUMMARY

In the third part of preparing for the appraisal, we will find that:

- Performance criteria need to be valid and meaningful. They will vary enormously from job to job, and for some jobs are very hard to specify objectively.

- Supervisor ratings can be a good way of obtaining data on the performance of the appraisee, but they must be designed with care.

- **Behaviourally-anchored rating scales** are one way of ensuring ratings are well-defined and accurately completed.

- The appraisee's previous objectives should be clearly related to actual performance; the general level of performance and particular successes and failures can then be seen at a glance.

- Psychometric tests can be a useful source of information for appraisals, particularly when information is needed about individual's potential. They include **ability, aptitude, personality, interests** and **motivation** tests.

- The choice of data depends on the type of job, status of job, and type of appraisal being carried out.

- A pre-appraisal report should contain all relevant data and a copy should be given to both appraiser and appraisee.

- Topics for discussion should be taken from the pre-appraisal report.

- Both parties should be clear about why appraisal is taking place and what is going to be discussed.

- The appraisal interview should follow a clear plan.

The data considered in this chapter differ from those considered earlier in that they are concerned with *the person doing the job* rather than with the job itself. That is, they are ways of assessing the person, both in terms of how they perform in the job, and in terms of their personal characteristics.

PERFORMANCE CRITERIA

Ideally, performance targets should be set using criteria that are **objective** and **fair**. How far this ideal is attained depends largely on the circumstances of the appraisal. Where data are unavoidably subjective, they should be carefully chosen and standardised across all employees.

It is crucial to the success of the appraisal to ensure that data is collected in a valid fashion. For sales staff the criteria may seem quite simple, the number or value of items sold in a given period. This seems objective enough. But it is not likely to be that simple. Other factors need to be taken into account, such as:

- size of sales territory
- number of customers
- number of potential customers
- experience in job
- type of items sold

These factors should be accounted for and the appraisee assessed in relation to other sales staff. The appraisee who sells the least number of items may in fact be the most effective performer because the territory is new, very small, and the number of potential customers limited. This illustrates the point that one should never form judgements on the basis of incomplete information, always incorporate **potential confounding factors**, such as size of territory and number of customers.

Data will often seem subjective when really it is objective and valid. A bricklayer can be assessed by the size of wall built, or the quality of the workmanship. The former is clearly objective data. The latter, if used carefully, need not be a subjective judgement as the accuracy of the bricklaying can be measured in terms of size of mortar joint, whether the wall is level or plumb, and so on.

Performance of managers

Thus we can view many jobs by carefully selecting and organising the data, but it's not always that easy. How do you measure the performance of a manager—by how he treats subordinates? (This could be measured using subordinate ratings.) Or by the number of tasks he does? How do you tell whether the tasks have been done efficiently, and how do you assess the value of each task? These problems might be solved using the job description, or by comparing performance with colleagues. For instance, does it take the appraisee longer to complete a task than his colleagues?

Thus for managers there will probably be a combination of objective and subjective performance criteria, the exact mix depending on the tasks involved. In this kind of job there are two very important considerations:

- The process of task analysis, job description and person specification described in the last chapter should be carried out thoroughly. This is an invaluable aid to obtaining the right performance criteria. The criteria will usually emerge during job analysis.

- The criteria that are chosen should accurately discriminate between the performance of efficient and inefficient managers. The appraiser wishes to know which people are performing best and why.

There is no simple answer to the question of how to assess performance in managerial jobs, but the question still needs careful consideration. It is not efficient to introduce subjective judgements (easy to obtain) simply because it is difficult to find objective data sources.

Supervisor ratings

One criterion commonly used for management (and many other kinds of job) is supervisor ratings. The supervisor is given a questionnaire to complete where the questions relate to the appraisee. The supervisor is asked to rate the performance of the appraisee on a number of factors using a numerical scale.

Ratings can also be obtained from peers and from subordinates where appropriate. The same rules as for the design of supervisor ratings largely apply, and so they are not considered separately here. There are some complications in interpreting these scales. Findings from peer ratings may be either artificially high or artificially low. They may be artificially low because of the effects of rivalry and jealousy, or colleagues may upgrade each other because they don't wish to be seen in a negative light by the interpreter of the scale. These effects may be removed if the rating scales are anonymous, though of course the problem may be exacerbated. The best results are obtained when there is a largish group of individuals being tested, who are all assessing each other. The distribution of scores for particular individuals on particular questions will provide useful information. If the distribution is relatively small, ie most people have rated an individual with the same score, then that score is likely to be accurate. Subordinate ratings involve similar problems to supervisor ratings in that any odd effects can be due to personality clashes. Also, subordinates may not want to be seen as criticising their superiors, but this has a lot to do with the culture of the organisation. Organisations that wish to succeed will accept the need for constructive criticism.

Criticisms of the technique
Supervisor ratings have been heavily criticised as a performance criterion, but this is largely because:

● they are badly designed
● they ask the wrong questions
● they have poor scales
● supervisors aren't trained to complete them properly.

These are important points. Fortunately they do not mean that supervisor ratings as such are useless. Properly designed, they can be very effective in all sorts of situations, and the results they produce can be reasonably (though never entirely) objective.

The right questions to ask
The particular questions that are used in the scale depend on:

● the nature of the job
● the person doing that job
● the purposes of the appraisal
● the nature of the supervision
● the amount of detail required from the supervisor.

The questions should be:

- carefully worded
- unambiguous
- not encouraging the supervisor to respond in one particular fashion
- not be so general as to be meaningless (eg 'Is X a nice person?').

You may need professional help in developing suitable supervisor rating scales, though this can be an expensive option and may only be viable in larger organisations. The following guidelines, if closely observed, will help you design good rating scales that suit your own organisation.

The rating system
Regarding the scales themselves, a five-point or at most a seven-point scale is usually most appropriate, ie:

Would you consider X gets on well with his/her colleagues?

Gets on very well				Gets on very badly
5	4	3	2	I

Any more than seven points and the difference between any two adjacent points becomes virtually meaningless. For instance, what does a difference between eight and nine mean on an eleven-point scale? Nothing. It is more or less impossible to make meaningful discriminations on such a scale.

The appraiser has to make sure the supervisor knows how to use the scales properly. Without training, there are big differences in the way people use the scales. On a five-point scale, some people will tend to use the middle of the range 2,3,4, never giving scores at the extreme. Others always use the extremes, effectively responding in a yes-no fashion.

- You have to ensure that supervisors all use the scales in a *similar* way, and that they all use the *full range* of scores available.

Behaviourally-anchored rating scales (BARS)
A more sophisticated way to improve rating scales is by using BARS. The major problem with normal rating scales is their lack of definition: what exactly does it mean to score 2 or 4? If

judgements are based instead on observable behaviour, these problems are overcome. The scale should contain a clear definition of the trait to be rated, eg friendliness. It should also have a description of the behaviours that can be observed at any level on a scale measuring that trait, eg 1 = always smiles at and speaks to colleagues and shows consideration to them, 5 = rather a sullen person, ignores colleagues and doesn't get involved in social activities.

BARS are put together by deciding the key aspects of job performance (from the job description), then developing 'anchors' by asking appropriate individuals to describe a number of critical incidents (see Chapter 5). These are sorted and assigned to each of the key aspects of job performance. Then the incidents are scaled and a rating scale is produced for each of the key aspects of job performance. The major problem with BARS is that they are highly job specific and expensive to produce, but they are more reliable and more valid than normal rating scales.

An example of a supervisor ratings questionnaire is given in Figure 4.

PERFORMANCE AGAINST PREVIOUS OBJECTIVES

Targets set at previous interviews should be included as part of the pre-appraisal report. They should be clearly related to *actual* performance so both appraiser and appraisee understand the general level of performance, as well as any particular successes and failures, at a glance. Targets are tied to the particular criteria that are used to determine performance. You can easily obtain the previously set objectives by referring to the previous appraisal report.

Targets for a salesperson might include total number of sales, number of new customers, number of repeat customers, average size of order, proportions of different products sold, plus whatever else is relevant to the organisation. These numerical figures can be put side by side with actual performance, and successes and failures will be easy to see. If the appraisee has failed to meet the target for new customers then the reasons for this can be discussed in the appraisal interview. Perhaps they were so busy with old customers there wasn't time to establish many new contacts, or few of the people approached wished to buy the goods. Whatever the reason, the areas for discussion are visible at a glance. An example of a form comparing targets with actual performance is given in Figure 5.

SUPERVISOR RATINGS QUESTIONNAIRE

Please complete the following questionnaire with regard to the performance of [Appraisee]. Please ensure you use the rating scale carefully, as you have been trained.
Return the completed questionnaire to: [Appraiser]
by: [Date]

How would you describe your relationship with X?

very friendly	1
friendly	2
cordial but with some formality	3
rather strained	4
very difficult	5

Would you say that X fits in well with his/her colleagues?

very well integrated into team	1
reasonably well integrated into team	2
there are sometimes problems between X and his/her colleagues	3
There are major problems between X and his/her colleagues	4

If you responded 3 or 4, please explain why. For instance, does X have problems with particular colleagues, or are there difficulties all round?

Does X generally have good realtionships with his/her customers and other contacts outside the organisation?

very good			very poor	
1	2	3	4	5

When X has a problem with work, does he/she approach you or some other appropriate person for help?

never   sometimes   usually   always

When X has a problem outside work that is affecting work, does he/she approach you or some other appropriate person for guidance?

never   sometimes   usually   always

Which of the following statements best describes X regarding his/her job?

very knowledgeable, keeps up-to-date on all developments	1
very knowledgeable about most areas of work	2
reasonably knowledgeable	3

there are some areas where X is not quite knowledgeable
enough   4
X is clearly not knowledgeable about many aspects
of his/her work   5

Is the overall standard of X's work:
very good	1
good	2
average	3
below average	4
poor	5

Do you often have to criticise X's work?
very often (daily)	1
often (every week)	2
average (every month)	3
sometimes (less than once a month)	4
almost never	5

Is X efficient with paperwork?

very efficient				very inefficient
1	2	3	4	5

Is X punctual in his/her production of reports, etc?
very punctual (never late)	1
reasonably punctual (about 1 in 10 late)	2
sometimes late (about 1 in 5 late)	3
often late (more than 1 in 5 late)	4

If you responded 3 or 4, do you know the reasons why the reports
are often late?

Can X work well under pressure?
very well	1
average	2
below average	3

Please rate X on the following characteristics on a scale of 1-5,
where:
1 = displays the quality in most relevant circumstances
2 = usually displays the quality
3 = displays the quality an average amount
4 = sometimes displays the quality
5 = rarely/never displays the quality

relationships with employers
decision-making

drive
initiative
self-control
interest in job
adaptability
personal appearance
punctuality
attendance

Please comment on any particular strengths and weaknesses X has in relation to work.

Strengths:
Weaknesses:

Do you have any suggestions for improvement?

Is it your opinion that X needs further training? If so, what type of training?

Please comment on X's overall performance.

Please add any further information you feel is relevant to this appraisal.

Fig. 4   Example of a supervisor ratings questionnaire

By using this form performance can be assessed at a glance, and areas where there are particular problems, or particularly good performance, can by readily determined. The original targets can be set by looking at the performance of the sales staff as a whole. Size of territory and number of potential customers are constants. If you have the completed form at the appraisal interview, then certain useful questions will soon emerge: Why is the value of goods per customer rather low? Why have there been too few new contacts? Why have few of the new contacts been turned into customers?

Forms like this can be designed for any job where objective data is to be had. They are particularly useful when 'confounding' factors have to be taken into account, such as the sales position described here. The important thing is to keep it simple. It is a way of simplifying complicated data to generate useful appraisal questions.

ATTAINMENT OF PREVIOUS OBJECTIVES: SALES PERSONNEL

Appraisee's name:

Position:

Appraiser's name:

Date:

Length of time in post (years):

	TARGET	ACTUAL
Number of customers	N	
Total value of sales	£	
Average value of sale per customer	£/N	
Number of new contacts	Co	
Number of new customers	Cu	
Proportion of contacts turned into customers	Cu/Co	
Size of territory	Ter	
Number of potential customers	pc	

Fig. 5   Comparing targets with actual performance

PSYCHOMETRIC TESTING

This is an area much neglected by appraisers. Many organisations fail to see the value of using psychometric tests on their employees. Though many may use certain tests for selection purposes, few are willing to extend this to the appraisal system as a whole.

This is unfortunate because psychometric tests, when used properly, can provide a lot of useful information both for the organisation and for the person being tested. You may not be qualified to select the particular tests required, but an expert can help you. The use of someone trained on a short course in psychometric testing will probably not be as efficient as using a trained psychologist, as the psychologist will have a background of practical knowledge that the non psychologist does not have.

The best use of psychometric testing

Psychometric tests aren't appropriate for all forms of appraisal. There is little point in using what can be quite expensive measures on appraisees who are simply having their regular performance review. There are two general areas where psychometric tests come into their own, providing information not readily available by other means:

● when you need to make predictions about future performance;

● where the appraisee wishes to find out more about their own future potential.

For example, tests would be appropriate in a promotion or transfer appraisal (predicting who is the best person for the job), and for use in assessing future potential, where tests of vocational interest can help the individual generate ideas for suitable alternative jobs.

Tests have an advantage over other forms of data, such as supervisor ratings; they are objective, standardised using large numbers of people, and unbiased (within realistic limits). Test results from properly validated, administered and scored tests are very reliable.

Scope of psychometric tests

Psychometric tests can measure a wide variety of areas. Going back to the person specification, they can indicate general intelligence and special aptitudes, interests, motivation and personality; ie, four out of the six points mentioned. They are relatively quick to administer (in relation to the information they can provide) and cost-effective.

Choosing the right tests from the ones available

Even if you need to enlist a psychologist to select appropriate tests, it is still useful to have some idea of the tests available. There are many tests on the market that are well presented, with glossy brochures and computer analysed output, but which have not been well constructed and standardised; so it is crucial to be able to tell good tests from bad. The tests are mainly of these types:

- ability tests
- aptitude tests
- personality questionnaires
- interests/values questionnaires
- motivation questionnaires

Ability tests
These include general ability or IQ (intelligence quotient) tests, which provide useful information about who has the potential to perform well. More detailed information about patterns of specific abilities (eg verbal, numerical, spatial) can be obtained using tests specifically designed for these purposes.

Examples
- What is the next number in the series: 1 3 7 15 31?

- Which is the odd one out: biron, porwspa, yenha, gelae

- In each row of words, find a word which means the same as or the opposite of the first word in the row:
    many: ill few down sour
    ancient: dry long happy old

Aptitude tests
These are designed to measure suitability for particular jobs, eg sales, mechanical, or supervisory roles.

Examples
- (Sales). Look at the following statements. Mark the one that is most like you with an M, mark the one that is least like you with an L.
    My selling is highly personal
    I am a conservative dresser
    I sometimes make price concessions to close a sale
    I have a good feel for people's reactions

- (Clerical). Coding   plastic 25
                         rubber 12
                         china 18
    Mark the correct response:
        rubber   25   12   18
        plastic 25   12   18
        china   25   12   18

Personality questionnaires

These provide valuable information about individual characteristics that can be matched to the person specification. They are
useful for assessing the appraisee's relationships with others (eg,
which personality characteristics are useful in a team) and how well
the appraisee will do the job. For instance, perseverance and
patience are needed by scientists, managers need to have leadership
qualities, sales staff may need to be extroverted.

There is the danger that this kind of test can be faked by
individuals to put themselves across in a more favourable light.
This can be partly offset in the design of the questionnaire, but
the effect of faking cannot be fully dismissed, and information from
personality questionnaires should always be used along with other
methods (interview, ratings, etc).

Examples

● Do you find yourself the centre of attention at parties?
    usually   sometimes   never

● Do people talk to you about their personal problems?
    often   sometimes   never

● Do you daydream?
    often   sometimes   never

Interest/values questionnaires

These help reveal an individual's basic interests and attitudes
across a wide area. How is the individual motivated? How suitable
is he for different kinds of jobs?

Examples
● Which job would you prefer?
        firefighter
        banker

● Mark the statement that is most like you (M) and least like
    you (L).
        to have a hot meal at noon
        to get a good night's sleep
        to get plenty of fresh air

Motivation questionnaires
These help determine what it is that motivates people, what drives them to act in the ways they do. Some basic motivators are money, job satisfaction, self-worth, and family.

Examples
- True wisdom comes through knowing yourself
  very true   true   false   very false

- Which of the following is the least reliable sign of success in a person's career?
  position of seniority
  rate of promotion
  reputation in the trade or profession
  salary

WHAT TYPES OF DATA SHOULD BE COLLECTED?

As noted earlier this depends on several factors—the type of job, its status, and the type of appraisal being carried out. Some examples have been given earlier regarding the use of particular types of data. A number of general remarks can be made.

Importance of current data
Firstly, it is *essential* that any job within the organisation has a current job description and person specification. This is not just for appraisals, it is to ensure that the organisation is efficiently staffed, that there are not too many or too few employees, that they are all in the right jobs, and that the jobs are all clearly defined. The job description and person specification should at all times be available to yourself as the appraiser so that:

- you are knowledgeable about the requirements of the job
- you are knowledgeable about the requirements of the person doing the job.

Job descriptions and person specifications are key sources of data when the appraisal concerns staff movement. This means promotion, transfer or selection (when the job descriptions and person specifications of both relevant jobs will be required), and when the appraisee need training.

The regular performance review will not need to consider the person specification in any depth if there are no particular performance problems. If there are, the specification can help show why objectives aren't being met. Compare the individual with the person specification and check for discrepancies. If the specification is accurate and the details of the individual are complete, this may well be where the problem lies. The regular performance review may only require measures of performance to compare with set objectives.

Supervisor ratings are useful for most appraisal purposes, though they will not always ask the same questions. For instance, if the appraisee is having vocational assessment, supervisor ratings need not consider present job performance in too much detail. They should concentrate instead on more general elements and on the personality of the appraisee.

As mentioned above, psychological tests are useful when the future behaviour of the appraisee needs to be predicted. These situations include:

● promotion
● transfer
● selection
● vocational assessment
● future potential

Psychological characteristics of individuals do not generally change in the short term. In theory general intelligence doesn't change at all and personality characteristics are fairly stable. So there is little point in measuring general intelligence or personality at the regular performance review.

The pre-appraisal report
Once all the relevant information or data has been collected, it should be condensed and put together in a **standard format report**.

Both you and appraisee should have a copy of this before the interview. It is important that *both parties* receive the same report. Detailed findings need not be presented at this stage. If the appraisee is given enormous piles of paper to read it may not get read at all, and simply create ill-feeling towards the appraisal. Detailed findings should be available in the appraisal interview in case they need to be referred to.

Too often in situations like this you will receive more information than the appraisee. This puts the appraisee at a distinct disadvantage. How can anyone give of their best unless they have equal access to all the information?

Keep it simple
The report should be simple in form, concise and intelligible to both parties. The information need not take up too much space. There are exceptions of course. An analysis of personality may take up several pages. Ideally the pre-appraisal report should just summarise the findings. The full report can be available at the interview if you need to discuss parts of it. It is important for such details to be open for discussion at the interview as the findings can be controversial.

Similarly, you don't need to include detailed results of supervisor ratings and other ratings. A general summary will do. In the appraisal interview itself you may need to refer to particular comments or ratings, so have these available. The purpose of the pre-appraisal report is to give both parties a general picture of the findings.

The report need not be more than one or two pages long, depending on the job and on the purpose(s) of the appraisal.

Prepare the ground in advance
It is important for both parties to receive the pre-appraisal report well in advance of the interview itself so that there is time to digest the contents and prepare responses. It is on the basis of this report that each party decides on the specific **topics** they wish to discuss, or the specific **questions** they wish to ask in the interview. This works both ways. The process is not an interrogation, though some appraisers might prefer it that way. The appraisee needs the information in order to be able to raise their own points.

Keep a flexible agenda
Appraisees may wish to raise issues that are not strictly 'on the agenda', that do not relate to the purposes of the appraisal as outlined at the outset. This should not deter them from raising the issue, for instance if the organisation is failing to provide adequate canteen facilities, or the work environment is in some way not conducive to health, or their career development is not being helped as they would wish.

It is useful to carry out a further exercise. Once each party has decided on the points they wish to raise in the interview, they should be listed and passed to the other party, so that person can

Case study: Psychometric testing

Daniel, managing director in a large computer manufacturing firm, wants to carry out a series of appraisals aimed at helping individuals plan their futures within the company. He knows that different types of people are suited to different types of jobs, but he doesn't have any information on how this would relate to his own company. To solve this problem he decides to enlist the services of a psychologist to look at how personality relates to effectiveness at different kinds of jobs.

Daniel arranged for the psychologist to test his staff over three days in one week. Using the results of the test and a measure of job performance, the psychologist would be able to work out which kinds of people are best suited to which particular jobs. The personality tests are duly carried out, the performance data collected, and the results interpreted. Unfortunately, it comes to light that many of the staff did not answer the questions truthfully (there were a number of 'lie questions' on the test), and so the results are invalid.

Daniel then decides to find out why people had manipulated the results. He finds out that people have been pushed into doing this test without being given any reasons why. A lot of people have assumed that the results are going to be filed and used against them when it comes to obtaining a pay rise or promotion. Because of this they deliberately tried to 'fix' the results to make themselves look good.

Comment
The problem for Daniel was that the employees hadn't been told before the test of the reasons for it. As soon as someone is asked to take a test they go on the defensive. If not told why they are taking it, they will assume the worst and (particularly with personality tests), they will answer in the way they think the employer wants them to answer.

think about their reply. As noted earlier, this system is used in Parliament to good effect, and can work just as well in the appraisal interview.

UNDERSTANDING YOUR OPPOSITE NUMBER

Before an effective interview can take place, it should be ensured that:

- each party understands the purposes of the appraisal;
- each party has a copy of the pre-appraisal report and has understood it;
- both parties know what issues they wish to raise;
- these issues have been given to the other party and that party has considered their responses.

Once all this has been done—and it need not be as difficult as it might appear—then each party will understand what the other wants out of the appraisal interview. This is particularly important to the appraisee. The interview need not now be something to look forward to with foreboding. Nervousness in an interview situation is something that arises partly out of ignorance about what will happen in the interview.

If the pre-appraisal report for a member of the sales staff contains information on sales performance, and they have failed to reach their targets, you would doubtless wish to raise this in the appraisal interview. If the appraisee is aware of this they can prepare their response. It may be that the poor performance is caused by factors not mentioned on the report such as poor quality samples. If the appraisee has time to think about it properly, he could bring along examples of the goods to show you.

PREPARING FOR THE INTERVIEW

The interview itself should follow a **predetermined plan**. Some appraisers may see this as an unnecessary chore. In fact, it is vital. Rambling interviews generally fail to provide the information required. They often amount to little more than informal chats with no direction or purpose. But for the appraiser who has got this far, who has determined the purposes of the appraisal, collected the data, and compiled a pre-appraisal report, it would be unwise not to consider the plan of the appraisal interview itself.

The appraisal interview consists of a number of stages, depending on the type of appraisal and the number of discussion points. Both parties should be well prepared for the interview, knowing exactly what is going to be discussed, so it should largely be a matter of deciding the order of the discussion points. The general plan should be like this:

1. The appraisal interview is usually different from the selection interview in that both parties are likely to know each other, so the first stage of setting someone at their ease will be different. It is still necessary to help the appraisee relax, as many are nervous about their appraisals.

2. Discuss any points arising from the pre-appraisal report. Cover these fully before moving on. It is crucial to let the appraisee raise any relevant issues they see as important.

3. Summarise the findings of the report and the discussion so far. Ensure that the appraisee agrees with this summary. This is important to ensure that both parties are still on the same wavelength!

4. Draw conclusions from the appraisal. For the regular performance review this will mean agreeing mutually satisfactory objectives for the coming period. Selection, transfer and redundancy appraisals will not have this type of conclusion because you will have to assess everyone before making any decisions. Only preliminary judgements will be made, and these must of necessity be kept from the appraisee.

Within this framework, the discussion of particular topics can be arranged in any sensible order, but don't lose sight of the fact that the appraisal interview is basically a conversation between two individuals with needs to be fulfilled, and particular styles of working.

POINTS FOR DISCUSSION

1. BARS provide a relatively objective measure of obtaining supervisors' ratings. From your own experience devise a relevant question and suitable behaviours that could be listed on each point on a seven-point scale.

2. If a psychometric test of aptitude was being designed for use on members of your team, what kind of questions do you think would be important?

3. Design a pre-appraisal report form that would be suitable for members of your own management team.

7
Conducting an Appraisal Interview

SUMMARY

In this section about the appraisal interview itself the main points to be considered will be that:

- The interview should take place at a time convenient for both parties, when the appraisee isn't busy.

- There should be adequate time set aside for the appraisal.

- The setting for the interview should be comfortable, and there should be no interruptions.

- The plan of the interview should be followed.

- The appraisal report should contain details of what has been agreed in the interview.

Once the preparation has been carried out the following should have been completed:

- The purposes of the interview have been decided.

- Appropriate data have been collected.

- The information has been passed across through a report.

- Both parties have been able to raise questions they wish to discuss in the interview.

The interview itself can go ahead.

INTERVIEW SCHEDULING

There are certain basic guidelines for carrying out interviews of any sort, including appraisals. The ones described below cover the most common type of appraisal, the regular performance review, and whatever other purposes this might incorporate.

Advance warning

The timing of the interview should be set well in advance so that both parties can fit their other work around the interview, and there are no clashes of appointments. The more notice that can be given, the more both parties will be prepared psychologically, and the less likely they are to be worried about 'what they are supposed to be doing', that is, what they call their 'real work'. This of course implies that appraisal is not part of their real work, but a chore to be got over with as quickly as possible and only if absolutely necessary, and certainly under protest. This book has tried to show that the appraisal is a crucial part of the effective functioning of the organisation. If the system is well designed and well publicised within the organisation, this particular problem should be alleviated.

Picking the right time

If possible, the meeting should be arranged for a **time** (of day, week, month or year) when the appraisee isn't likely to be busy. This isn't always possible but often it is. For example, a mince pie sales executive should not have his appraisal in the last few months before Christmas, the most hectic selling time for mince pies. Neither should the appraisal be carried out just after Christmas, because there probably won't have been time for the organisation to have collected the sales performance figures for the lead up to Christmas. Perhaps March or April would be a good month: after the rush, after the figures have been compiled, but before the next season gets underway. Other jobs, instead of having busy times of the year, have busy times of the month, week, or day. The same rule applies: try and fit the appraisal into a quiet period. It will help the appraisee stop worrying about the work that has to be done. It will also ensure a minimum loss of productivity.

Upsetting the appraisee's normal work routine should be avoided as much as possible, but it should be emphasised that, in the end, the appraisal *is* really part of the normal work routine. It is an integral part of the employee's activities.

Allowing time for preparation

Do ensure that there is adequate time before the appraisal date to prepare properly. Complex facts and figures cannot usually be gathered in a few days. It may take weeks, especially if job descriptions have to be devised. On the other hand, the time span shouldn't be too long. It is of little use the appraisee thinking about the appraisal for months, as this may affect their job performance. Appraisal is, and should be, a psychologically demanding exercise for the appraisee. Preparation of the kind described in this book should minimise the stress but there is little point in increasing it again by giving the appraisee too long to think about the appraisal. For a regular performance rewiew, the appraisee will know more or less when it is to take place, because it will fall at regular intervals, perhaps the same month every year. But active preparation, from date setting to data gathering, should not start too early.

How long should the interview be?

The appraisal interview itself needs to be given a long enough **time slot**. Don't try to cram it into a half-hour lunch break. If the interview is too rushed the parties may be unable to cover all the points they wish to raise, and important ones will be skimmed over or missed out entirely. The appraisee may come away frustrated for lack of time to discuss a particular point. This could be a serious demotivator.

The length of the interview will depend on what has to be covered, but it is very unlikely that few but the most basic appraisals—the simplest regular performance reviews—can be carried out in much under an hour. An average session that covers everything it is supposed to, in the detail required, will probably last more like two hours. On the other hand, if the interview lasts much longer than two hours the participants would probably start to lose their concentration. When setting the date and time for the interview, take this into consideration.

If the guidelines described in previous chapters have been followed, there will be quite a lot of contact between yourself and the appraisee before the appraisal interview. This will establish the ground rules, what the appraisal is for, and what will happen during the interview, what will be discussed and so forth. Even if you don't know each other before, you should know each other quite well before the interview takes place.

THE PLACE OF INTERVIEW

The appraisal interview should be carried out in a quiet warm room, with comfortable chairs, and drinks (not alcohol!) available. Avoid interruptions by visitors or telephones. The image of the appraiser sitting behind a big desk and the appraisee cowering in front of it on a lower chair should be avoided. Confrontation does not help communication. The appraisee may feel cowed and you may find it difficult to forget your power status. The best position is sitting not quite opposite each other, with at the most a low table between you both to put papers on.

CONDUCTING THE INTERVIEW

Both parties should ensure they have the pre-appraisal report to hand, marked with points they wish to discuss. They should both have notes of specific points they wish to raise. Most people cannot be expected to rely on memory to recall all these topics. Both should also have paper on which to jot down points of importance.

The actual structure of the interview cannot be given in detail as (a) different people favour different approaches, and (b) different types of appraisal need different plans. The intent here is to provide general guidelines.

The structure of the interview

The interview should start with a short informal chat on general topics not related to the appraisal, just to ensure both parties are relaxed. The interview proper should then begin with points arising from the pre-appraisal report. From this the discussion can broaden to include the other topics to be covered, perhaps the appraisee's strengths and weaknesses, opportunities and problems, achievements, under-achievements, ideas for changes, and possible future objectives. These points should be summarised and agreed, conclusions should be drawn and the session amicably closed.

Points to bear in mind

Certain things need to be kept in mind during the interview:

● Firstly, what are the purposes of the appraisal? At all times these should be kept in mind and the appraisal should not be allowed to stray from them. This is your responsibility; if you feel that the interview is straying guide it back on course.

● The interview should progress at a sensible rate and cover the issues it is designed to cover. Though issues must be covered in sufficient detail, there may be times when a point is being laboured and little progress made. Control must then be regained (your responsibility) so that the interview can move on to the next point.

- Notes can and should be made by both parties throughout. Afterwards these will form the basis for the appraisal report. Both of you should jot down points discussed, agreements reached and action to be taken. Also note where agreement could not be reached.

- A clear record should be kept of the appraisee's agreed performance objectives for the coming period. It is essential to avoid confusion here. The objectives should be clearly laid out, translatable into sensible performance criteria (so an assessment can be made later), be unambiguous and, crucially, achievable.

Communicating with the appraisee

There are almost bound to be some points on which you and the appraisee fail to agree. If this is on performance objectives, an area where there has to be agreement in the end, there should be recourse to a *referee*, someone who can adjudicate and decide what the objectives should be. This person should be someone respected by both parties. It should not be the appraiser, because if you have the ultimate power of decision then the bargaining power of the appraisee will be diminished from the start. The appraisee may lose confidence and trust in you, damaging future relationships. It may still be difficult sometimes, because it could seem to the appraisee that he is powerless, and that objectives are being ordered from above. Of course, this may be necessary in some cases, but avoid it if possible. If the appraisee thinks he has little or no say in the work he has to do, motivation will drop and with it productivity. The individual is important.

You may be in a position to propose action to be undertaken, such as training, but you may not always be able to authorise such action without referring to higher authority. Never make promises you can't keep. If an action has to be authorised by someone else, tell the appraisee this. Explain that you will make a recommendation but that the decision will be made by this third person.

Bear in mind throughout the value of **praise** and **criticism**. During the discussion, whenever it is shown that the appraisee has done something praiseworthy, then use praise. It is a great motivator. On the other hand, when the appraisee has done something poorly, then be critical, but constructively so. Don't just say 'Your performance was poor', say 'Your performance was poor. I think it is because of XYZ. What do you think?'. The appraisee will accept criticism more readily if it is constructive. If the criticism is not supported by evidence the appraisee is likely to resent the organisation and feel unfairly treated. This will lead to lower productivity.

By the close of the interview, all discussion points should have been covered in a way acceptable to both parties. As far as possible, the purposes of the appraisal should have been met, conclusions should have been agreed, such as setting objectives for the coming year or agreeing on the appraisee's training needs. The interview should end amicably, even if there have been heated discussions on some matters, and even if agreement wasn't reached on one or a number of points. There is nothing to be gained by taking anger or animosity away from the meeting.

THE APPRAISAL REPORT

As soon as possible after the appraisal interview, either you or the appraisee should complete the appraisal report. This report should contain details of:

- the purposes of the appraisal
- points discussed
- conclusions reached
- objectives set
- matters that remain unresolved.

The report should then be shown to the other party, who can check it and see whether they agree with the content. There should be space for them to add their own comments, regarding something that has been omitted, or something they disagree with. The report is then signed to show that both parties approve it. It is then forwarded to whoever is authorised to see it, such as the personnel director, the employer, or the person responsible for training. Both the appraiser and the appraisee should keep a copy, and a copy should be filed for future reference by authorised persons.

The appraisal report is traditionally written by the appraiser, but this does not have to be so. If both parties agree the findings of the interview, then a report written by the appraisee has two distinct advantages:

● it acts as a motivator to the appraisee, who is given a real chance to express him or herself and whose views are being taken seriously;
● it ensures that there hasn't been a misunderstanding between the two parties.

Value of the report for future reference

The appraisal form can be used for reference in future appraisals, as long as it is used with care. It is sometimes argued that previous appraisal reports shouldn't be used in this way in case there is an adverse effect. In other words, if the appraisee performed poorly in the past, then the person who appraises them next will be biased and more likely to judge the appraisee as doing badly now. As long as care is taken to not make this kind of judgement, by training appraisers assessing data more objectively and not over-emphasising the importance of past performance to present performance, the use of previous appraisal reports can be helpful. They act as on-going indicators to judge whether the long-term progress of the individual is satisfactory.

Confidentiality

There will unfortunately be times when the appraisal report has to contain information that the appraisee cannot see. These should be kept to a minimum as secrecy does not help trust. But there are cases where need overrides openness, for instance when the appraisal is for selection or promotion purposes. Here you may have to add a final section after the appraisee has seen the report, that contains specific information and recommendations for who-ever is making the selection or promotion.

Figure 6 is an example of an appraisal report. It gives an idea of how one might be structured, but the actual layout will depend on the specific needs of your organisation and the type of appraisal being carried out. If the appraisal concerns promotion, then there will need to be a section on whether or not the appraisee is considered suitable. If the appraisal is to assess future potential, there will need to be a section on possible career paths and job roles.

The appraisal report format

The format of the appraisal report is very important. Rating scales

APPRAISAL REPORT
Pro forma appraisal report form for the purpose of annual review.
   This report should be completed as soon as possible after the
completion of the appraisal interview.

Name of appraisee:
Position:
Name of appraiser:
Date:

Performance:
1. Job knowledge
thorough knowledge of   5   4   3   2   1   inadequate knowledge
all aspects of job   of job
Comments:

2. Organisational skills
outstanding organiser   5   4   3   2   1   very poor organiser
Comments:

3. Leadership qualities
a consistently outstanding   5   4   3   2   1   avoids the
leader   responsibilities of
                                                     leadership
Comments:

4. Resourcefulness
very resourceful   5   4   3   2   1   lacks originality
Comments:

5. Attendance/punctuality
excellent time-keeper, never   5   4   3   2   1   often late without
absent without a good reason   good reason
Comments:

6. Ability to delegate
exceptional   5   4   3   2   1   poor
Comments:

7. Counselling skills
exceptional   5   4   3   2   1   poor
Comments:

8. Competence in handling disciplinary matters
very competent   5   4   3   2   1   lacks competence
Comments:

9. Assessing subordinates' training needs
very capable   5   4   3   2   1   not at all capable
Comments:

10. Motivating others
excellent   5   4   3   2   1   poor
Comments:

11. Financial competence
very competent   5   4   3   2   1   not competent
Comments:

12. Communication skills
oral: strong   5   4   3   2   1   weak
written: strong   5   4   3   2   1   weak
Comments:

Personal Qualities
13. Judgement
excellent   5   4   3   2   1   very poor
Comments:

14. Reliability under stress
very good   5   4   3   2   1   very poor
Comments:

15. Cooperation with others
excellent: 5   4   3   2   1   weak
Comments:

16. Appearance and bearing
smart   5   4   3   2   1   slovenly
Comments:

Recommendations
Particularly strong areas:
Particularly weak areas:
Training needs:
Future potential:
Signed (Appraiser):   Date:

Appraisee Comments
I have read the above report and have the following comments to
make.

Signed (Appraisee):   Date:

Fig. 6   Example of an appraisal report

are useful because they allow rapid assessments to be made of individuals, and comparisons between individuals. The comments section on each point should always be fully completed. Anyone who then reads the report will see why the appraisee has obtained that particular rating.

The format suggested above is only one possibility. Some appraisers or organisations may prefer a more qualitative report, with open-ended questions and comments by the appraiser on more general aspects of the appraisee. Examples of sections in such a report include:

- Is the appraisee an effective worker?

- Does the appraisee have any immediate or longer term training needs?

- Does the appraisee get on well with their colleagues?

- Does the appraisee have any work or relevant personal problems?

Note the word 'relevant' in the final point. It is *not* the place of any appraisal to interfere in the private lives of individuals. The only time the organisation has authority to consider an individual's personal problems is when they are interfering with work.

The information given under each section of a qualitative appraisal report should be fairly detailed, one or two paragraphs in length.

The format of the appraisal report can be arranged in any way from purely rating scales to purely qualitative comments. Both have their pros and cons. Some combination of the two will probably be right for most organisations and most appraisal purposes. Rating scales are easy to interpret and compare across individuals, but they can only contain limited information and are fixed before the appraisal, so not allowing for unexpected results. Qualitative reports can provide a lot of information, but can be difficult to interpret and compare across individuals in an objective way.

Case study: When should the interview take place?

Emily has been called in for her appraisal interview at a particularly busy time. She has received a number of unexpected orders and is under pressure to complete them quickly. On top of the normal pressures associated with rush orders, the shop floor staff are creating difficulties regarding their overtime pay and bonus scheme. They want the bonus to be set at a higher rate than usual to compensate for the extra work and extra hours worked.

Emily, understandably, does not want her appraisal at this time. She prefers to wait a few weeks until things have calmed down, but 'the powers that be' have set the date and the time and they will not alter it.

In many ways the appraisal system of Emily's company is a good one. It is standardised across the organisation to ensure fair comparisons between individuals in different departments, and the main review appraisals are carried out by trained staff from the personnel department. Unfortunately there are drawbacks. The system is very rigid and it doesn't allow for situations like Emily's, an unexpectedly busy time. The appraisal system has its own schedules to meet and postponing interviews is seen as a problem to be avoided if at all possible.

Because Emily is under such pressure, her appraisal does not go well. She is ill-prepared and the discussion fails to achieve anything significant. Targets cannot be set, as Emily is not in a position to comment on them. Emily wants to discuss her future, as she hopes to obtain a promotion in the near future, but again this proves to be impossible because her mind is on the problems in her department. Finally, the appraiser has to agree to another interview at a more convenient date for Emily, so in the end a great deal of time is wasted, both Emily's and the appraiser's.

POINTS FOR DISCUSSION

1. Look at the way you conduct interviews. What are your own strengths and weaknesses as an interviewer? Make a list. Try to look at it from both your point of view and that of the interviewee's.

2. Where do you presently conduct interviews? Is this a good place? Why/why not?

3. Design a suitable appraisal report form for your own management team.

8
Follow Up, Validation and Conclusion

SUMMARY

This chapter will suggest that:

- Any recommendations for action made in the appraisal interview should be followed up quickly.

- The appraisal system needs to be constantly validated. Detailed records must be kept, and the same appraisal system used throughout the organisation so that comparisons can be made.

- Ways of validating the system include: asking the participants for their thoughts, checking whether the system predicts future performance, and analysing the completed appraisal reports.

- Unfairness should be avoided. Unfairness includes stereotyping, relying on first impressions, acting on false assumptions, the halo effect.

- Conflict can arise in the appraisal interview: via the appraisee, the appraiser, or the organisation itself.

- The twin purposes of appraisal systems are to optimise individual job satisfaction and organisational efficiency.

- If the organisation satisfied the needs of the individual, the individual is likely to satisfy the needs of the organisation.

An efficient appraisal system does not end with the appraisal interview. There are two further issues to be considered, two important elements to ensure continuity for individual job satisfaction and cost-effectiveness. These are:

- how appraisals should be followed up
- how the system should be validated.

The chaper ends with a look at two further issues of importance to individuals and organisations involved in operating appraisal systems. These are: firstly, reasons why appraisals might be unfair; secondly, sources of conflict.

HOW APPRAISALS SHOULD BE FOLLOWED UP

Any recommendations for action that are made must be followed up. If the conclusion is that the appraisee needs training, then the right training should be provided as soon as possible. There is little point in offering a training course that is needed immediately and then not providing it for 12 months. That may save the cost of training, but it is potentially 12 months extra productivity wasted, and that productivity should be worth far more than the cost of the training.

This is particularly true in jobs where there is rapidly changing technology. For instance, a computer programmer will need regular training to keep up-to-date on the latest programming languages. It is widely acknowledged that an organisation which fails to keep up with changes in technology is likely to fall by the wayside, but there is little point in keeping up with technology if your employees don't receive appropriate training. Appraisal will ensure that training keeps pace with changes in technology.

Recommendations

If you have only been able to *recommend* training to an authorising person (employer, personnel manager), then make your recommendation quickly, for the reason given above. If for some reason your recommendation is not supported, and the authorising person refuses to fund the training, then the appraisee should be given written notice of this, including the reasons why it was refused. Then, if the appraisee wishes to, they can appeal against the decision. After all, the decision to recommend training will have been made on detailed objective data, after careful discussion. The appraisee has a right to know the basis on which the authorising person has made their decision. It may be that funds for training are just not available. If so, then it is better to let the appraisee know than to let him think that the organisation doesn't value him as an employee worth training. If the appraisee thinks this his performance will suffer.

Keeping records

Keep a continuous record of whether performance targets are being attained. Depending on the work being done, this might be a weekly record of objectives set against achievements. This record will encourage appraisees to try to reach targets, and provide useful data for the next appraisal. The supervisor should check this record regularly. Any potential difficulties should be spotted as early as possible, and put right before they get too serious.

The record form should consist for example of a checklist of tasks to complete, a sales target to reach, or number of items to produce, where the appropriate category can be marked as achieved and the standard at which it has been completed can be shown.

The importance of follow up

By following up all the recommendations of the appraisal, the organisation will show the individual that he/she is important to it. The appraisal is designed to prove this, by not only assessing performance against objectives, but also by assessing individual needs and then providing for these needs.

It is crucial that there is **continuity** for the individual and for the organisation in the appraisal system. Of course, this doesn't fully apply to all forms of appraisal. Selection and transfer, for example, have continuity in the way they are carried out, but in the organisational rather than the individual sense. But continuity is a fundamental part of, for instance, the regular performance review. The appraisal is an integral part of the appraisee's work life. Using data from repeated appraisals, performance is assessed over the long term.

The appraisal ensures that the organisation has up-to-date information about the jobs being done and the people that do them. For the appraisee it is a way of knowing that their career is being monitored to make sure it is being developed to the full.

VALIDATING YOUR SYSTEM

Once an appraisal system has been introduced using the guidelines presented in this book, it should not just be used when needed and never examined to check whether it is working properly or not. A car will develop faults if its working parts aren't adjusted or replaced when necessary. It is the same with an appraisal system. Over time it becomes outdated, through changes in jobs, changes in people and new ways of doing things. This is why your system should be continuously **validated**.

The same basic appraisal system should be used throughout your organisation so that comparisons can be drawn between employees' performances. This does not mean that every appraisal will be the same. Firstly, as we have seen, appraisals with different purposes are put together in different ways, using different types of data. Secondly, individuals are not the same. They will bring their own idiosyncrasies into the design and running of the appraisal. This should not be discouraged, as long as it is kept within reasonable limits, and bias and subjective judgement are minimised.

Appraisals must be carried out in the most efficient manner and the conclusions they draw should be useful both to the organisation and to the individual. Objectives should be attainable, the right person chosen for training, the right person promoted, the individual given job satisfaction. The only way to ensure this is constantly to review the system to see what should be changed, where any faults lie and where improvements can be made.

Validation should be an *on-going* process set up at the same time as, and as part of, the appraisal system. This will help dispose of any teething problems. The appraisal system should have regular 'services', it should be validated regularly to ensure it is running smoothly. Over time the organisation changes: in size, structure, the make-up of its employees, its products, its overall philosophy. As these occur, modify the appraisal system as necessary. Regular checks on the system will ensure its continuing efficiency.

How to validate the system

In order to validate the appraisal system, detailed **records** need to be kept. These are the standard records that any efficient organisation will keep. They should consist of each employee's **personal file**, including information on background (CV, original application form), history within the organisation (posts held, absenteeism), performance targets and achievements (whether all targets have been attained, if not why not), training and qualifications (job-related academic qualifications will be in background information), and any further relevant data. There should also be detailed and regularly updated job descriptions and person specifications for each job.

The organisation should have someone in the role of **second**

APPRAISAL VALIDITY QUESTIONNAIRE—APPRAISEE

Appraisee's name:
Position:
Appraiser's name:
Date:
Date of last appraisal:
Purpose(s) of last appraisal:
Name of appraiser:

Please rate the following on a scale of 1 to 5, where:
1 = very unacceptable
2 = unacceptable
3 = barely acceptable
4 = acceptable
5 = very acceptable

Rating

The preparation of the appraiser
Your preparation time
The pre-appraisal report
The interview:
     did it cover all the necessary issues?
     was it conducted in a professional manner?
The appraisal report
Follow-up

Please answer the following questions in full.

Are you happy with the way the appraisal system is set up?
Are there any general improvements you would like to see?
Did you receive adequate notice of your last appraisal?
Were you happy with your appraiser? Was he/she prepared
     properly for the appraisal?
Did you have enough time to prepare?
Were you happy with the pre-appraisal report?
Was the interview conducted in a fair and professional manner?
Were you happy with the appraisal report? Was the rating fair and
     consistent?
Did you get appropriate action on anything promised in the
appraisal?
Do any of the report forms need to be changed or improved?
Please add any general comments you would like to make.

Fig. 7   Appraisee's appraisal validity questionnaire

reviewer, who is knowledgeable about all aspects of the appraisal system and who can carry out the validation.

There are various methods of validating the system. Four essential ones are considered here:

- ask the appraisees whether it is working
- ask the appraisers whether it is working
- assess whether the system predicts performance
- analyse the completed appraisal forms.

Asking the appraisees

The first two methods involve using a standard questionnaire (different for appraisee and appraiser—see below). This should contain questions about the competence of the appraiser, whether the information obtained before and during the interview was complete and accurate, whether performance objectives were set at a reasonable level, and perhaps most importantly, whether intended actions arising out of the interview were followed up rapidly and efficiently. An example of a questionnaire that might be given to the appraisee is shown in Figure 7.

The combination of quantitative scales and qualitative comments should get the maximum information from the appraisee. Action should be taken on any question where the appraisee has expressed discontent. This may mean interviewing the appraisee to find out more details, interviewing the appraiser, or looking at report forms.

Asking the appraisers

The questionnaire designed to be completed by the appraiser is slightly different from the one administered to the appraisee. An example of such a form is shown in Figure 8.

Does the system predict performance?

The next validation method involves checking the various types of data. If the ways of collecting data are valid, then they should predict what they are supposed to about employees. For instance, supervisor performance ratings should correlate to more objective performance criteria (such as sales figures, productivity); psychological tests should predict future performance.

Predictive validity is useful when the appraisal system is used for job changes, transfer or promotion. Records are kept of the appraisee's predicted performance. Predictions are made by using data such as psychological test scores, ratings on previous job, productivity on previous job. At some point in the future (perhaps

APPRAISAL VALIDITY QUESTIONNAIRE—APPRAISER

Appraiser's name:
Position:
Date:

Details of appraisals carried out in last month:

Date   Appraisee's name   Purpose of appraisal

Continue on a separate sheet if necessary.

Please rate the following on a scale of 1 to 5, where:
1 = very unacceptable
2 = unacceptable
3 = barely acceptable
4 = acceptable
5 = very acceptable

The ratings are for general comments relating to appraisals carried out in the last month.

                                                              Rating

Time available for preparation
Access to relevant data
How well the appraisee has prepared
Site for interview
Pre-appraisal report form
Appraisal report form
Follow-up

Please answer the following questions in full:

Did you have enough time for preparing the appraisals?
Is obtaining access to necessary information difficult (eg difficulty in finding records, obtaining help with the design of supervisor rating scales)?
Are the appraisees generally well prepared for the interview?
Can you always obtain a suitable room for the interview?
Are there any changes you would like to see to any of the appraisal forms?
Have all follow ups you have recommended been carried through?
Please add any general comments you would like to make.

Fig. 8   Appraiser's appraisal validity questionnaire

a year hence), actual performance on the new job is measured. A correlation is obtained between predicted and actual performance. The higher the correlation, the higher the validity of the appraisal system (or at least that aspect that predicts future performance). In this way predictive validity is extremely valuable.

Analyse the completed appraisal forms
This involves checking the appraisal forms to ensure they are being completed in a standardised manner. There should be no bias between different appraisers, or against certain individuals. This method of validation also looks at whether the information they contain actually helps the organisation and/or the appraisee. The responses on the appraisal form should not contain judgements that are unfair to any individual, nor any irrelevant information.

The second reviewer should interview a sample of appraisees, using the completed appraisal form, working through the whole form section by section to ensure the appraisee is satisfied with what is written. The interview should also cover any topics on the validity questionnaire felt by the appraisee to be unacceptable.

The second reviewer will be able to pick out other problems by comparing a sample of reports. **Biases** can occur between departments and between appraisers, and these can be assessed easily enough. The second reviewer should take a sample of reports from each appraiser (or each department) and work out averages and score distributions of the rating scales. If there are differences in how the appraisers are using the rating scales, they will emerge from this analysis.

For instance, if one appraiser regularly rates appraisees using 3, 4 and 5, then their average may be around 4. A second appraiser rates at 2, 3 and 4. Their average may be around 3. This difference between the two appraisers is quite large, and would need action to resolve. If the problem isn't resolved, and if at some stage a comparison is made between two appraisees, one from each of the above appraisers, an unfair advantage will be had by the appraisee who was assessed by the first appraiser.

Regarding **score distribution**, the second reviewer should make sure all appraisers have a similar distribution of scores on the rating scales (see Chapter 6). If one appraiser tends to use extreme ratings (1 and 5) and another uses the middle range (3,4,5), then apparent but misleading differences will exist.

Whichever methods are used, it is essential to keep complete and accurate records for use in the validation procedure.

Validation is just as essential a part of the appraisal system as any other part. Without proper validation, there is no way of telling whether the system is working efficiently. If it isn't, then its value is diminished, both for the organisation and the individual. If records are accurate and frequently up-dated, and validation is part of the normal procedure, then it will be cost-effective.

WHY APPRAISALS CAN BE UNFAIR

Unfairness can arise at any point in the appraisal system. It is essential to try to minimise unfairness.

Even those people who consider themselves extremely fair-minded have many biases and prejudices about one another and towards ideas. This can affect how the appraisal works. If we didn't classify people using **stereotypes**, which introduce systematic bias and prejudice, then we would find it difficult to put order into the way we look at the world. Stereotyping is the process of grouping essentially heterogeneous people into homogenous categories, such as the employee who is a member of a union being seen as a potential trouble-maker when there is no evidence for this. This is unfair.

Unfairness is in many cases trivial, but it can sometimes lead to serious consequences. Common stereotypes include **race, sex role**, and **social class**.

First impressions
Linked to these is the notion of 'first impressions'. The first time we meet people we have a psychological need to classify them as quickly as possible. So we latch on to a particular characteristic, or look, and link that to ones that, in our personal view of the world, belongs to some stereotypical group. Once that characteristic has been identified, then the person is assumed to have all the other characteristics of that stereotype.

Example
To take a simple and rather unsubtle example, a manager may wrongly imagine that anyone with a non-standard accent is lower in intelligence, tends to have less educaton and has poorer leadership qualities than someone with a standard accent. Though the manager may not *consciously* think in this way, they may *act* on the stereotype in the appraisal and, perhaps, fail to suggest that the appraisee is put forward for promotion. This manager is behaving in a way common to us all, that is, we act on *assumptions* that we have made without our even knowing that we have made them.

This sort of problem can be avoided when acting in the role of appraiser—or for that matter the appraisee—by careful analysis of the data available about a person, not the 'data' that you are inventing because you are using stereotypes. Awareness of stereotyping and its effects can itself reduce these effects because we can learn to act solely on the objective data, not our subjective judgements.

The halo effect
Another form of unfairness is called the 'halo effect'. This occurs when you know that the appraisee has done particularly well in one area of work, and so you assume that all other areas of the job are being done just as well. For instance, the appraisee may have done an excellent piece of work and received a bonus for it. You may fall into the trap of noting this particular piece of work and emphasising it so much that other areas of performance are ignored. But this may be the only bit of very good work the appraisee has done, and there may be real problems in other areas.

The appraisal interview shouldn't just concentrate on praising the good work; it should also bring out the reasons for poor performance so that something can be done about it. Perhaps the appraisee in the above example, acting quite naturally, will try to concentrate discussion on this good piece of work to avoid being questioned on failings in other areas.

The halo effect also works in reverse. An otherwise competent individual may be over-criticised because of a single shoddy piece of work. Again it can work over the long term. The individual may get an unjustified reputation as a poor worker. This has the added danger of turning into a **self-fulfilling prophecy**. If the individual is viewed by others as incompetent, then this perception itself may cause him or her to perform incompetently.

SOURCES OF CONFLICT

No matter how open, fair and equal the appraisal system is designed to be, power games may be played between the two parties, who can often see themselves in some sort of organisation versus employee conflict. Power games occur in appraisals because the roles of the appraiser and appraisee as 'boss' and 'subordinate' are temporarily suspended; both parties may be vying for position in the 'equal' roles.

Conflict arises from certain other sources:

Case study: Follow up

Mark's appraisal had been quite useful, or so he thought immediately afterwards. He had discussed with Martin, his appraiser, a number of problems he has had recently. Mark works for a car manufacturer that believes in a broad-based training for its junior managers. Following this philosophy, Mark has recently moved from production to sales to widen his experience. Unfortunately, he has found it hard to adapt. He is nervous when meeting new people, often making mistakes in what he says. This didn't matter in production, even though he was meeting people all the time as they were usually the same people. In sales it is different, Mark has to meet new people every day, and if he makes a mistake he may lose a sale.

The first three months were not very good in comparison with other new members of the sales staff. Martin was very sympathetic to Mark's case in the appraisal and they both realised something needed to be done about it.

'Assertiveness training, that's what you need', said Martin. Mark agreed. This was included in the appraisal report, to be carried out as soon as possible.

After the appraisal, Mark carried on making mistakes in his work, improving little with practice. He was waiting for the training, but it didn't come. He contacted Martin, who said, 'I'm sorry. I'd informed personnel, they should have dealt with it. I'll get on to them straightaway.'

Mark again waited and nothing happened. Again he contacted Martin, who again apologised and promised to 'get it sorted out'.

Mark eventually waited six months before he finally got the training, by which time he had wasted six months in a job he didn't like and wasn't very good at. By the time he had the training it was time for him to move on, and so any benefits gained from the training would not benefit sales.

Comment

This situation shows how easy it is for action promised at an appraisal not to happen. The firm has a very good management programme that involved training and broad job experience, but in this instance it failed due to a lack of communication between the relevant departments. The potential loss is significant. Apart from the loss of sales in the period Mark did not have his training, there is the possibility that he will become disillusioned with the company and either fail to live up to his potential, or find a job elsewhere with a company that keeps its promises.

- Within the appraisee, who may fear that the object is to decide who to dismiss, or who to withhold bonuses or pay rises from.

- Within the appraiser, who may believe the appraisee is trying to hide information.

- Within the organisation itself, the climate of which may foster conflict more than cooperation.

Confict does not help the effective appraisal system. Appraisals should be run in a spirit of cooperation rather than conflict, with both parties working together to solve problems.

Designers of appraisal systems need to find ways of minimising potential conflict, and one good way is via training. If both parties are aware of possible sources of conflict, and how they harm the process, they are more likely to try and avoid them.

CONCLUSIONS

If the guidelines laid out here are followed, then the appraisal interview will perform a useful function within the organisation. On the other hand, appraisals have little value if they are not designed properly. If they lack validity the organisation will simply be throwing its money away; it will be wasting time and resources on a system that doesn't do what it is supposed to do, that is, optimise organisational efficiency and individual job satisfaction.

On the other hand, if the appraisal system is well designed it can provide much useful information for the organisation on all sorts of topics, from assessing performance in the regular performance review to choosing the best candidate for promotion.

The appraisal is used as a method of assessing individual performance within the organisation. There are two main purposes: to ensure that the right person is in the right job and doing it to a suitable standard, and to ensure that the person doing the job has a high degree of job satisfaction and fulfilment. Too many appraisals have only considered the first purpose, perhaps paying lip-service to the second. In modern society there is a growing awareness of the value of people long-term, that they mean much more than short-term profit, for the successful functioning of any organisation, though there is no reason why we should not have both.

● If the organisation satisfies the needs of the individual, the individual will satisfy the needs of the organisation.

POINTS FOR DISCUSSION

1. In your own organisation, how could follow up procedures be made more effective?

2. What would be the best ways of validating an appraisal procedure in your own organisation?

3. In what ways could you minimise unfairness in your own appraisal procedures?

9
More Case Studies

This chapter consists of a series of case studies illustrating appraisal systems in different organisations. Each case study consists of:

- Summary task analysis, job description, and person specification forms.

- An outline of the appraisal system in use, including its good and bad points, and how it might be improved.

The jobs included here are chosen to illustrate a variety of roles. The issues discussed apply to most, if not all, jobs. The jobs are:

- veterinary nurse
- workshop foreman
- accounts clerk
- technical manager
- dairy operative
- supermarket cashier

VETERINARY NURSE

Task Analysis
Job title: veterinary nurse
Company: Elmingbury Veterinary Hospital
Date: 2 September 1992
Supervisor's name: all partners of practice
Appraiser's name: Helen Robinson (veterinary surgeon)

Task	Knowledge skills	Aptitudes	Personality
Pre-operation preparation	anaesthesia sterilisation		practical

Assisting in surgery	theatre nursing	manual dexterity	attention to detail
Post-op care	general nursing		cope in emergency
Laboratory analysis	basic scientific skills	observation analytical	patience
Ordering drugs	drug knowledge	clerical/arithmetic	
Take/develop X-rays	radiology		conscientious
Field trips	general nursing		practical adaptable
Reception	filing	clerical	friendly sociable

It will be seen from this task analysis that not all categories are completed. This is largely because particular characteristics cannot be stated for many tasks. The important thing is that *all* the tasks the nurse does are included in the list, and any **essential skills**, aptitudes or personality characteristics are included.

Job description
Job title: veterinary nurse
Department: NA
Responsible to: head veterinary nurse
Responsible for: trainee nurses
Number employed on this work: 8
Position from which candidates for this job might come: none internal, usually school leavers
Avenues of promotion: head veterinary nurse
Purpose/objects of work: to assist veterinary surgeon in all aspects of her work, especially in the preparation, care and after care of animals.
Main duties/activities: general veterinary nursing, laboratory, surgery, drug dispensing/ordering, dealing with enquiries.
Forms/equipment: order book for drugs, case history cards, veterinary care equipment.
Contacts: daily contact with team of veterinary surgeons, nurses, members of public.

Discretion: can vary only within limited parameters, determined by instructions of veterinary surgeons.

Checking: frequent, carried out by all veterinary surgeons.

Supervision required: receive daily instructions on diagnostic matters. All such decisions are the sole responsibility of veterinary surgeon.

Supervision given: limited authority to assign general duties to trainee nurses.

Other responsibilities: on call evenings and weekends on rota with other nurses. Delivery and collection of animals and laboratory samples.

Working conditions: two years training, rate of pay on qualification £3.80 per hour basic.

Personal requirements: practicality, common sense, hard-working, acceptance that veterinary nursing is a way of life.

The task analysis has helped the appraiser design the job description, though information from other sources is also used, such as personnel records and information from the veterinary surgeons. The appraiser, by combining the information from the task analysis and the job description, can now complete the person specification.

Person specification

Essential	Desirable	Conflicting
Qualifications		
3 GCSEs	English Language Biology	
Intelligence/aptitudes		
average general ability	manual dexterity clerical aptitude analytical	
Personality		
common sense	cheerful	fear of blood/dirt
practical	stable	tender-minded
hard-working		absent-minded
Interests		
animals	people	
biology		

Motivation

love of animals   money
caring

Appearance/circumstances

few family pressures   concern with looks

How the appraisal system works

The appraisal system for the veterinary nurses in this hospital
consists of a regular performance review every six months, and
appraisals for other purposes as and when required. As it is a small
organisation, most appraisals are carried out on an informal day-to-
day basis. This does not obviate the need for the regular formal
review. Appraisals for the nurses are all carried out by the same
veterinary surgeon (who is responsible for all general personnel
issues), and they are spread through the year so she isn't overloaded
with too many appraisals at once.

This is a reasonably good system for an organisation such as this.
Assigning responsibility for the appraisal to a single veterinary
surgeon is useful because it makes for consistency in how the
interviews are carried out, as long as the appraiser is fair to all the
nurses. It is particularly useful to have performance reviews every
six months because most veterinary nurses are relatively young
females whose lives may be changing rapidly.

In small organisations appraisal of staff is carried out just on a
day-to-day bases, with *no* formal interview. While this saves a great
deal of time in a busy practice, it may mean that the practice is
not making the best use of staff, and staff discontent may go
unnoticed until it is too late.

The data collected for the performance review consists of a
supervisor questionnaire, obtained from all the veterinary
surgeons. Each surgeon is asked the same series of questions,
specifically:

- Is the appraisee efficient in surgery?
- Does the appraisee competently carry out all her duties
  regarding pre- and post-operative care?
- Does the appraisee carry out her other duties efficiently
  (X-rays, field trips, laboratory analysis, etc)?
- Are there any areas where the appraisee is deficient? Could
  this be rectified by further training?
- Is the appraisee's general attitude to work acceptable?
- Have you any general comments to make about the appraisee?

This questionnaire is short, which is very useful because veterinary surgeons typically do not like filling in forms. One problem that may arise is that the appraiser is one of the surgeons. This is a problem typical of smaller organisations, where **objectivity of judgement** is difficult because everyone knows each other very well and there may be personal favourites and petty animosities. The appraiser must remain objective by taking into account the general views of the veterinary surgeons. As data is obtained from all the veterinary surgeons, any personal dislikes should be alleviated by the general picture.

The problem with this kind of data is that it is difficult to make clear judgements. The surgeons will seldom all make exactly the same comments about a particular appraisee. The appraiser has to be careful to form a balanced judgement about the appraisee's need for training, or her general competence, or her attitude to work.

It may be more efficient if the supervisors were asked to fill in rating scales regarding these questions. It would certainly make it easier for the appraiser to draw conclusions about the views of the veterinary surgeons. Behaviourally anchored rating scales would be best, to obtain the maximum consistency of judgement.

There is no standardised appraisal report form. Any comments made by the appraiser are simply entered on a piece of paper in the appraisee's personnel record file. This piece of paper rarely includes any comments made by the supervisor, or any of the appraisee's own comments, but simply any conclusions drawn by the appraiser.

Clearly, there is a need for an appraisal report form that is standardised and thus comparable between appraisees. It should contain details of work performance as assessed by the supervisor questionnaire, plus:

- details of any objectives, both organisational and personal, for the coming period
- details of the conclusions reached by the appraiser after the interview
- a section for any comments the appraisee wishes to add.

The form should be signed by both the appraiser and the appraisee to ensure it has been read and accepted by both.

However, this appraisal system is not validated in any way. A second reviewer should therefore be appointed. This would be one of the other veterinary surgeons, who can ask the appraisees whether they are satisfied with the system, and check the conclusions drawn by the appraiser from the supervisor questionnaire.

Unfortunately, though the appraisal system works reasonably well for the other nurses, the head nurse rarely receives her performance review. The veterinary surgeons do not see the need for it. She has been with the hospital for a number of years, starting as a trainee nurse and working her way up. The veterinary surgeons are perfectly happy with her performance, and, as she has never complained, they assume she is happy in her work. This type of assumption can be dangerous, as there may be underlying problems that develop over time, relating to work or personal life.

A problem that could emerge is that the head nurse is unable to obtain promotion within the organisation. The only way to obtain more status would be to move to a larger veterinary hospital. If the veterinary surgeons are happy with her performance they should ensure she has enough job satisfaction to want to stay. This may mean altering her conditions of service, perhaps a pay increase, reducing her hours of work, changing the tasks she has to do, or (if she has a family) reducing the time she has to be on call at evenings and weekends. The best way to ensure she isn't becoming dissatisfied is not to wait for her to say so—she may never say anything—but to hold a formal review appraisal where this type of problem is discussed as a matter of course.

Conclusion

Although the hospital has a reasonable appraisal system, there are some relatively minor changes that could improve it considerably. They would not be too expensive or time-consuming to introduce, but they would lead to considerable benefits to the practice.

WORKSHOP FOREMAN (CAR MECHANIC)

Task analysis
Job title: foreman
Department: workshop
Company: Banders of Bletchley
Appraisee's name: Geoff Priggen
Supervisor's name: Daniel Johnson
Appraiser's name: Richard Kilburn

Task	Knowledge/skills	Aptitudes	Personality
Maintenance of vehicles	City & Guilds Motor Vehicle Technology	mechanical manual dexterity	
Supervising technicians		leadership motivating verbal	sociable
Diagnosis of faults		analytical	patient

The task 'maintenance of vehicles' covers a host of tasks, from routine servicing of vehicles, to changing engines, to bodywork repairs. For this particular job the City & Guilds qualification assumes that the individual will be competent in all these tasks. 'Diagnosis of faults' is included as a separate task because it involves an intellectual aptitude, analytical ability, that is not crucial to simply maintaining vehicles. Of course, a mechanic will always be involved with diagnosing faults, but it is useful to have this separate category so the appraiser can see in which areas particular abilities are needed.

Job description
Job title: foreman
Department: workshop
Responsible to: service manager
Responsible for: 6 workshop technicians
Number employed on this work: 1
Position from which candidates for this job might come: workshop technician
Avenues of promotion/transfer from this position: service manager
Purpose/objects of work: maintenance of motor vehicles and diagnosis of faults
Main duties/activities: as above, plus supervision of technicians and quality control check
Forms/equipment: quality control forms, use of diagnosis machinery
Contacts: constant contact with technicians, daily contact with service manager, regular contact with public
Discretion: assigning duties to technicians
Checking: work is checked weekly at random
Supervision required: none
Supervision given: assigning and checking work of technicians and dealing with minor disciplinary problems

Other responsibilities: dealing with complaints from public, ordering parts, checking machinery, auditing

Working conditions/conditions of service: training for the basic job of technician is three years. Supervisory status is only obtained after a number of years shop floor experience. The post is salaried, £15,000 a year

Personal requirements: City & Guilds qualification in motor vehicle technology. Self-reliant, sociable, practical.

Person specification

Essential	Desirable	Conflicting
Qualifications		
City & Guilds	GCSEs	
Intelligence/aptitudes		
manual dexterity	analytical	
mechanical		
Personality		
resourceful	sociable	absent-minded
	patient	
Interests		
mechanical		
Motivation		
Appearance/circumstances		
smartly dressed		

There is no comment under 'motivation' as the person in this job need not be motivated by any of the usual things—money, status, friends, etc. In cases such as this, where there are no definite characteristics to be included, the space should be left blank, as including something that is not relevant will be misleading.

How the appraisal system works

The appraisal system at Banders of Bletchley (a garage which is part of a national chain) covers all technicians, including the workshop foreman. The service manager carries out appraisals annually. The data used for the general technicians consist of written comments provided by the workshop foreman. The interview for the workshop foreman is quite informal; the appraiser doesn't bother obtaining any data beforehand, and the interview itself is little more than a friendly chat. The only problems the service manager knows about concerning the foreman are those he has heard 'on the grapevine'.

Clearly, the appraisal system at Banders has a number of faults. While the supervisor doesn't actually carry out the appraisals of the technicians, he is responsible for providing all the data the appraiser will use. If he has problems in his relationships with any of the technicians, there may be an adverse effect on the way he writes the comments. This is a very subjective and one-sided way of collecting data. The appraiser should, as well as obtaining supervisor ratings, assess the technicians on other measures of performance: number of mistakes made, time taken to complete tasks, interaction with the public, and so on.

The appraisal for the workshop foreman is worse. This is not really an appraisal at all. It is just an informal chat. If the foreman has anything about his performance to hide, he will probably succeed in doing so. There need to be other ways of obtaining data, ratings from the technicians (subordinate ratings), number of mistakes made, etc.

In order to improve the appraisal system and the overall functioning of the garage, the appraiser should introduce **standard methods** of assessing performance. Records should be kept of how all the technicians, the foreman included, perform. These forms can include measures of, for instance, number and type of errors made, and time taken to complete work.

The results of the appraisal are not shown on a standard form to be referred to at a future date. The appraisal report form is essential, as the results of the interview are only known to the appraiser, and if they are not recorded they will be forgotten. The standard appraisal form need not be very long, with questions relating to:

- performance measures
- explanations of good/poor performance
- future objectives
- needs of the appraisee.

The garage is part of a national chain, but there is no standard appraisal system used throughout the chain. The responsibility for appraisals is left solely to the service manager. As attitudes of service managers will vary enormously, standards of appraisal at different garages will vary in a similar fashion. If individuals wish for promotion within the organisation, perhaps via transfers to other garages, some will be at an unfair disadvantage simply because their service manager showed little interest in appraisals, and so produced very little performance data on the employees.

Conclusion
The appraisal system in this organisation needs a thorough overhaul at national level. There should be a common policy for appraisals (formal appraisals, with objective ways of collecting data, standard report forms, etc), and service managers should undergo thorough training in appraisal techniques.

ACCOUNTS CLERK

Task analysis
Job title: accounts clerk
Department: accounts
Company: Street & Co
Appraisee's name: Cherilyn Heale
Supervisor's name: Jane Oldfield
Appraiser's name: Stephen Claxton

Task	Knowledge/skills	Aptitudes	Personality
General accounts	basic accountancy	numerical	
Customer liaison	workings of company		sociable friendly
Word processing	typing/shorthand	manual dexterity	conscientious
Reception telephone			polite

Job description
Job title: accounts preparation clerk
Department: computer room
Responsible to: John Street (Partner)
Responsible for: NA
Number employed on this work: 3
Positions for which candidates for this job might come: accounts department, purchase/sales, ledger clerks
Avenues of promotion/transfer from this position: none within organisation
Purposes/objects of work: monthly/annual analysis of accounts

Main duties/activities: preparing and inputting accounts, reception, word processing, customer liaison

Forms/equipment: IBIS computer, WordStar word processor

Contacts: daily with partners, other staff, daily with customers

Discretion: none. All work produced to standard format

Checking: all work double checked by other clerks, and also partners

Supervision required: all work authorised by one or other partner.

Supervision given: all staff in computer room on same level, advice and help given to each other as and when required

Other responsibilities: typing letters, producing reports

Working conditions/conditions of service: full time or part time, basic accountancy skills and typing required. Rate of pay £4.50 per hour basic, depending on age, qualifications and experience.

Personal requirements: GCSEs, GCEs, including English Language and Mathematics. RSA II, basic accountancy.

Person specification

Essential	Desirable	Conflicting
Qualifications		
RSA II	accountancy	
	GCSE maths	
	English language	
Intelligence/aptitudes		
arithmetical	verbal	
Personality		
conscientious	conforming	self-indulgent
	sociable	
Interests		
	business	
Motivation		
	personal esteem	
Appearance/circumstances		
smart appearance		

How the appraisal system works

The appraisal system for Street & Co is virtually nonexistent, except in the sense of the day-to-day running of the organisation.

This consists of informally checking any errors made (through the double checking system mentioned in the job description), and who makes them. If someone appears to be making 'too many errors' (an undefined quantity) then one of the partners will talk to them to find out why. If one of the accounts preparation clerks has a personal problem that is affecting work, or wishes to discuss anything, the only system that exists is for them to try and catch one of the partners in a free minute.

Clearly, the appraisal system at Street & Co is not very efficient. As it is only a small organisation there is no personnel department as such, nor is there a single person responsible for personnel issues. This needs to be rectified. One (or more) of the partners should take on the responsibility for personnel issues such as recruitment, appraisal and personnel records.

The partner might object that this would take up too much of their valuable time. They need to realise that their employees are valuable too. Once a system is established, it need not take up very much time, perhaps one morning a week at the most. Unfortunately the time taken to set up the system will be quite significant. This is what puts many employers off. If none of the partners can really take time off to organise the new personnel system, then outside help can be obtained in the form of a management consultant, not just any management consultant, but one experienced in personnel issues, especially appraisal.

Conclusion

There are a number of key changes to be made at Street & Co. Firstly, employee records and job descriptions need to be organised and kept up to date. The organisation first needs the means of collecting relevant performance data—for accounts clerks this will be number of errors made, speed of working, typing speed, supervisor (partner) ratings. The appraisal system can then be organised.

A company like this might need regular performance reviews every 12 months, with a constant check kept on performance throughout the year. The regular performance review needs to include:

● target performance
● actual performance
● a discussion of any discrepancies between actual and target performance
● appraisee grievances

- opportunities for self-development
- any other matters.

An appraisal form should be designed to incorporate these sections.

The appraisals should all be carried out by the partner responsible for personnel issues. All the appraisals should be carried out around the same time of year, so that after the results of the interviews have been obtained all the partners can meet to discuss the findings: what training should be offered, whether anyone's duties should be altered, whether the organisation is running smoothly, whether everyone is satisfied with their work, and if not why not.

TECHNICAL MANAGER

The technical manager is 35 years old, and has been working with the company for two years.

Task analysis
Job title: technical manager
Department: technical
Company: Vargenpane
Appraisee's name: Chas Roberts

Task	Knowledge/skills	Aptitudes	Personality
Supervising technical staff	general management skills	leadership	self-assured flexible assertive
Quality control	chemistry	observation	experimenting
Advising end-users	product knowledge	verbal	sociable
Reporting to MD	departmental knowledge	verbal	self-assured relaxed
Communicating with other departments		verbal	sociable
Internal and external audits	BS5750		attention to detail

Staff appraisal	interviewing counselling	verbal numerical	adaptable mature
Presentations	public speaking	verbal	confident relaxed
Product development	chemistry consumer	analytical	patient experi- menting

This task analysis is necessarily only a summary as the technical manager can be called upon to attend to a very wide variety of tasks, including all those normally carried out by subordinates, in addition to his usual tasks.

Job description
Job title: technical manager
Department: technical
Responsible to: managing director
Responsible for: personal assistant, product development manager, R & D technicians, QC team leader, QC technicians, trainees
Number employed on this work: 18
Position from which candidates for this job might come: chemical industry
Avenues of promotion/transfer from this position: directorship, operations, marketing
Purposes/objects of work: to coordinate and supervise the operation of the technical department
Main duties/activities: supervisory, customer services, improving existing standards/products, conducting internal and external audits
Forms/equipment: working procedures, quality manual, quality control specifications, chemistry laboratory equipment
Contacts: daily, with all departments, suppliers, distributors, end-users
Discretion: rarely receive written/oral instructions from directors. Methods of work, order of tasks can be varied quite considerably
Checking: no regular checking. Weekly meeting with MD to discuss work, and any errors made
Supervision required: none
Supervision given: responsibility for assigning/checking work, performance assessment, discipline, and dealing with grievances.

Involved with recommending appointments, transfers, promotion, and discharges. Can provide performance bonuses within a previously agreed budget.

Other responsibilities: market research of products

Working conditions/conditions of service: office, staff canteen. £19,000 + car.

Personal requirements: degree in chemistry, managerial and supervisory skills, knowledge of BS5750.

The task analysis and job description have given some idea of the breadth of knowledge and skills required in the job of technical manager, along with some desirable personality traits. The kind of individual that fits the post is determined using the person specification.

Person specification

Essential	Desirable	Conflicting
Qualifications		
Degree in Chemistry	Chemical engineering	
Intelligence/aptitudes		
verbal	numerical	
scientific		
writing		
Personality		
self-sufficient	relaxed	immature
confident	attentive	tender-minded
leadership	sociable	dependent
Interests		
	practical	
	administrative	
Motivation		
dedication	status	
Appearance/circumstances		
Smart, clean	nights away	

The section with most information is personality. This is because good managers need certain characteristics that enable them not only to be competent at the jobs carried out by their subordinates, but also to have the personal and leadership traits that enable them to succeed.

How the appraisal system works

The appraisal system for Chas is very informal. Basically, it consists of the weekly meeting with the MD mentioned in the job description. There is supposed to be a formal appraisal system in operation, but in the two years he has been there, Chas has never had such an appraisal.

The weekly meeting with the MD is quite thorough as far as the job is concerned. The discussions cover the performance of the department in general, what has been achieved and what needs to be achieved. The meeting acts as a check that the department is acting in line with company policy. Chas himself is not directly appraised, except in the sense that if there are any mistakes in his department, he is the one who gets the blame.

An appraisal such as this ensures that all departments are kept in touch with company policy (the MD meets all departmental heads individually, once a week), but it does little to help the individual manager. It is implicitly accepted that the meeting will only consider issues of performance, not any problems Chas may be experiencing. If Chas does have a problem, he can't discuss it at the meeting because it 'isn't the right time or place'.

There is clearly a need for a *formal* appraisal system that will take into account the needs of individual managers, not one that is rumoured to exist, but one that actually functions.

The appraisal system for subordinates is at the moment virtually nonexistent. Though the company is relatively small, employing around 250 people, there is no company policy regarding appraisals. Each department head is expected to organise his or her own appraisal system. Chas has been trying to do this for some time, but is put off by a number of factors. Firstly, before taking this post he had never expected to do appraisals. He had never been trained to do them, he wouldn't have known where to start. In the last two years he has tentatively attempted a few appraisals when the need arose. For instance, an opening arose in the marketing department that he thought might suit one of his staff, so he arranged an appraisal meeting with her to discuss her possible transfer to the marketing department. The interview did achieve some success. Chas found out that Caroline was bored in her present job—but she didn't want to go into marketing. Instead,

Chas has tried to develop her present post to open up new opportunities. Another appraisal has been arranged for six months' time to see if the new arrangements are working.

Because there is is no formal appraisal system, Chas would not otherwise have found out that Caroline was dissatisfied in her present job. She wasn't the type to complain.

Chas has found other obstacles in his way to setting up an appraisal system for the technical department. Because he has no formal knowledge of, or training in, appraisal he has contacted other departments which he knows do run appraisals to find out what they do. Unfortunately it is very difficult to get information from them. They are always too busy, or shrug it off with a comment like: 'Well, you just interview everyone and ask if they're getting on all right'.

Chas is well aware that this isn't the best way to carry out appraisals. The technical department needs several different types of appraisals. These include:

- promotion/transfer; these already happen to some extent but they could be improved by introducing objective data
- regular performance review, which should use objective means of assessing performance
- guidance appraisals, where employees can discuss any problems and needs they may have.

Conclusion

In summary, the company would benefit from a systematic appraisal system that would include training potential appraisers such as Chas, and encourage formal appraisals for all levels of staff.

DAIRY OPERATIVE

The operative is 31 years old, and has been working with the company for six months.

Task analysis

Job title: dairy operative
Company: Fast Foods Ltd
Appraisee's name: Bob Reid

Task	Knowledge/skills	Aptitudes	Personality
Cheese bagging		manual dexterity	
Bag sealing			
Weighing	reading/writing		
Crating		strength	
Stacking		strength	

The task analysis contains relatively little information because of the unsophisticated nature of the tasks involved in the job. Particular personality characteristics are not really relevant for any individual task, though as we shall see, some may be relevant to the job as a whole.

Job description

Job title: dairy operative

Department: cheese packing

Responsible to: production supervisor

Responsible for: NA

Number employed on this work: seven

Position from which candidates for this job might come: other departments, external

Avenues of promotion/transfer from this position: cutting room, mixing room, loading bay, laboratory, supervisor

Purposes/objects of work: packing cheese

Main duties/activities: five separate tasks on production line from bagging the cheese to transferring it to despatch

Tasks worked on rota system

Forms/equipment: air bagging, vacuum, weighing machines

Cheese weight log

Contacts: daily with supervisor

Discretion: no discretion to vary methods of work. Oral instructions

Checking: supervisor and self

Supervision required: once trained, very little. Breakdown of equipment referred to supervisor

Supervision given: NA

Other responsibilities: NA

Working conditions/conditions of service: sterile environment, non-smoking, clean overalls every day. Showers and canteen provided. Learning of job requires approximately 30 minutes per task. 12-hour shifts (6 till 6 alternate nights and days). Tasks rotate every two hours.

Rate of pay £5 an hour plus regular overtime (over 8 hours) and night premium.

Personal requirements: no particular educational qualifications. Aptitudes: manual dexterity and strength.

Person specification

Essential	Desirable	Conflicting
Qualifications none necessary		* see note
Intelligence/aptitudes manual dexterity		
Personality high boredom threshold	sense of humour	
Interests		
Motivation money		
Appearance/circumstances clean		

* For any routine job such as this, that involves little variety, there is a tendency to think that any educational qualifications are 'conflicting'. The reality is that the right personality traits are more important. The operative must have the ability to 'switch off', to think about something other than the task that they are doing—once it has become automatic.

How the appraisal system works

The appraisal system for Bob entails very little. As is often the case with factory work the employer places a lot of emphasis on production and little on staff morale. Virtually the only thing that is actually designed to relieve the boredom of the staff is the job rotation system, whereby the operators change tasks every two hours. Bob's workrate is constrained by the rate at which cheeses are sent along the conveyor belt, one every 11 seconds.

The only formal appraisal Bob has received and is likely to get is the induction appraisal. This took place about two months after he started with the company. During these two months Bob had a variety of duties in different departments; mixing, cutting, packing and loading. As most processes (except loading) are automated, performance is measured on error rates, that is, the number of times the process is delayed because of operative error. The company has a cut-off point for overall performance during this probationary period. If the operative falls below this point employment is terminated. The department to which the operative is sent depends on the needs of the company and the job at which the operative is most efficient. Little consideration is given to the employee. Bob did well enough on most tasks and the company needed an operative in the packing department, so without any consultation he was sent there.

Bob is constantly appraised in the sense that error rates are continually monitored. If he was to fall below the cut-off for that department he would receive a warning.

Conclusion
This appraisal system could be improved by taking into account the views of the operatives. To encourage people to work the company has a generous bonus package, but this assumes that people are motivated mainly by money. This is true for some, but other factors are also important. Because the job is boring, repetitive work, it could be improved by rotating the operatives between departments, perhaps weekly. A further improvement would be to have regular appraisals with operatives to tell them how the company is doing and what it is proposing for the future. This kind of appraisal, showing the employee you are interested in them as a person, works as an effective motivator for even the most boring of jobs. It cuts labour turnover and increases productivity.

It will be seen that appraisals for this kind of assembly line work, where the individual is little more than an extension to the machine and has to conform to precise work practices, are very difficult but not impossible. Though they will not be very sophisticated they will still be of benefit to both company and employee.

SUPERMARKET CASHIER

Gillian is 30 years old and has worked as a cashier for five years.

Task analysis
Job title: cashier

Company: Betterbuys
Appraisee's name: Gillian Rose
Supervisor's name: Kevin Lesley

Task	Knowledge/skills	Aptitudes	Personality
Till operating	till operations cheque handling returns/refunds	numerical	pleasant polite, helpful relaxed
Shelf filling			
Stock taking	numeracy/literacy		attention to detail
Weighing fruit/veg			
Serving on food counter	types of food	judging weights	friendly disposition

Job description
Job title: cashier
Company: Betterbuy
Responsible to: checkout supervisor
Responsible for: NA
Number employed on this work: 23
Position from which candidates for this job might come: external
Avenues of promotion/transfer from this position: checkout supervisor
Purpose/objects of work: to serve customers
Main duties/activities: operating till, stocking shelves, serving on food counter, weighing fruit/vegetables, stocktaking.
Forms/equipment: checkout tills, refund forms, stock inventories, weighing scales
Contacts: regular daily contact with: supervisor, manager, customers, other cashiers
Discretion: little scope to vary methods of work. Oral instructions from supervisor and manager
Checking: till receipts checked daily
Supervision required: on tills, all difficulties referred to supervisor, including wrongly priced goods, unpriced goods, problems with tills, cheques, alcohol (if cashier under 18)
Supervision given: none
Other responsibilities: responding to customer enquiries

Working conditions/conditions of service: shifts varied between 0800-2000. Basic pay, £2.90 an hour (trained), overtime available. Part-time or full-time. Staff canteen.

Personal requirements: basic literacy/numeracy, cleanliness, smart appearance, cheerful disposition.

Person specification

Essential	Desirable	Conflicting
Qualifications		
	GCSE Maths/English	
Intelligence/aptitudes		
	numerical	
Personality		
friendly/honest, polite/helpful		aggressive
Interests		
	people	
Motivation		
		status
Appearance/circumstances		
clean, smart		

How the appraisal system works

The cashiers at Betterbuy have a reasonably good appraisal system. They all join as trainees, usually for six months, during which time they are trained in all the tasks involved, under close supervision. At the end of this period they are appraised. This appraisal has two aims, to ensure they are happy with their work before being promoted to fully-trained cashier, and to ensure they are doing well at all tasks.

The appraisal system also calls for a regular performance review every year. This is the responsibility of one of the assistant managers. The purposes are to consider the appraisee's performance, their own feelings about the job, and their potential for promotion.

Performance data consists of a written report from the supervisor and error rates on the till receipts.

Gillian's last appraisal showed her performance to be excellent, with consistently good supervisor reports. The management wanted her to apply for a supervisor's position. At the appraisal interview Gillian felt rather pressured, and though she didn't want the job she applied for it and got it. It quickly went wrong. She found the new responsibility difficult, and after only four months asked to go back to her previous job.

Conclusion

This illustration shows the importance of carrying out appraisals properly. The appraiser made the basic mistake of assuming that someone who was good at one job would be good at another one. The promotion appraisal should have included an assessment of Gillian's potential as a supervisor, particularly her potential for taking responsibility. The appraiser should have been wary from the start as she didn't really want the job in the first place.

SUGGESTED PROJECTS

1. Design an appraisal procedure for the accounts preparation clerk.

2. Design an appraisal procedure for the technical manager.

3. Take an example of the way you currently appraise an individual, or the way you are appraised yourself, and put it in the format of the above case studies. Highlight the problems or potential problems with the procedure.

Glossary

Appraisal. The process of estimating the value of an individual to the organisation through regular assessment. There are a number of purposes of appraisal, including reviewing performance, assessing training needs and making future plans. Apart from assessing how well the individual meets the needs of the organisation, the appraisal should be assessing the organisation to determine how well it meets the needs of the individual.

Appraisee. The individual being appraised. All employees of an organisation should be appraised regularly.

Appraiser. The individual carrying out the appraisal. This role can be fulfilled by the line manager, the supervisor, or a specialist from the personnel department.

Aptitude. An ability relating to a specific task or area of knowledge to do with the job (eg sales aptitude, mechanical aptitude).

Bias. Acting more favourably towards one person or group than another without good reason. Bias can arise in the individual or be an integral part of the appraisal system (ie biased interviewer or biased data). Simply having the knowledge that bias exists can help reduce its effects. Validation of the appraisal system should determine how much bias exists. It is crucial to try and avoid bias, though this is sometimes very difficult, both because much of the data collected relating to many jobs is subjective, and also because many appraisers and appraisees know each other and work together on a day-to-day basis.

Career development. One primary aim of the appraisal for appraisees is to ensure that their future within the organisation is being properly planned, that it is going in the right direction. Appraisals are opportunities for individuals to express any dissatisfaction and to suggest alternative courses of action (eg transfer or retraining).

Communication. The act of conveying information between two parties. Effective communication in the appraisal is essential. All relevant information should be received at the right time by both parties, whether verbal or written.

Conflict. Conflict or opposition is unavoidable in many appraisals, whether it is related to the job, eg how it is being done, or to the person, eg whether the two parties get on well together. The word 'opposition' implies that two parties have separate ideas and, for whatever reason, fail to communicate.

Correlation. A statistical technique used to determine the degree of relationship or association between two variables. The closer the relationship, the higher the correlation. A perfect correlation is represented by +1.0, a perfect negative correlation by -1.0. If there is no relationship at all, this is represented by 0.0.

Counselling. Counselling is being used by more and more organisations as they recognise it has a number of essential puposes, from reducing stress to the analysis of personal problems. Counselling means listening to the individual, sympathising with their situation and helping them solve their problem in their own way.

Data (objective/subjective). Data are the raw kinds of information collected for and used in the appraisal. Objective data is quantifiable, ie can be turned into numbers. Subjective data is more controversial. It is non-quantifiable and is thus more liable to bias and problems of interpretation.

Discrimination. This refers to the differential treatment of groups of people, with prejudicial connotations. Society is still having difficulty ridding itself of the various kinds of discrimination, for example race, sex, sexual preferences, age. It is important that the appraiser does not introduce bias in the appraisal system through discrimination. Apart from being unethical and diminishing the validity of the system, it may also be illegal.

Feedback. The appraisee should receive information relating to his or her performance not just after the appraisal interview, but throughout the year. Feedback should be constructive, and should consider where performance is good (praise/reward) as well as poor (criticism/punishment).

Follow up. The concrete results of the appraisal, specifically where decisions are made to take action of one sort or another (training/transfer, etc).

Future potential. What is the individual likely to achieve in the future? In which areas are they likely to be successful? An appraisal assessing future potential is often carried out shortly after an individual joins the organisation to see how to best satisfy both individual and organisational needs.

Intelligence. General mental ability, as opposed to specific aptitudes. Intelligence in this sense is not concerned with the individual's skill in any particular area of knowledge, but with a general ability to carry out a range of intellectual tasks. The measurement of general intelligence (sometimes known as IQ) can predict performance in many situations.

Interview. Interviewing is used in any situation where people wish to receive and give verbal information in an orderly fashion. Interviews can be one-to-one, as in most appraisals, or many-to-one (or panel) as is the case for many selection interviews.

Interviewing skills. The success or otherwise of the interview depends on the type of questions asked and the responses they elicit. Interviewers should give a lot of thought to the questions they will ask in the interview, and ask questions that are going to produce the most information without distressing the interviewee. The interviewee should similarly prepare for the interview, both by preparing answers to questions they think they will be asked, and by thinking of some questions they themselves wish to ask.

Job analysis. A job is dissected into its component parts using task analyses, interviews with staff, personnel and job records, so as to determine the structure of the job. The job needs to be fully understood when designing an appraisal system.

Job description. All jobs should provide an accurate, detailed, and up-to-date job description so workers are clear about their duties and responsibilities. The job description should make the job-holder's position and responsibilities within the organisation clear.

Job redesign. This involves restructuring the job, perhaps after problems have emerged through job analysis. Tasks may be altered, added, or removed in order to create a more coherent structure and maximise the efficiency and satisfaction of workers carrying out the job. It should be carried out in consultation with job-holders, supervisors, and anyone else involved in the job.

Job satisfaction. In previous decades, organisations have focussed on maximising productivity. Now they are more likely to emphasise the welfare of the employee. This in turn benefits the organisation. If an individual is to give of his best, he should have satisfaction in the job.

Leadership. Leadership is crucial to organisational success. The best leaders share certain personal qualities; they tend on the whole to be sociable, extroverted, considerate towards others, assertive, and intuitive. They are not necessarily more intelligent than the rest of the team, but they can create and maintain group cohesion and give direction and purpose to group activities. But effective leadership is more than having the right personal qualities, the ethos of the organisation is also important.

Listening skills. These are crucial to any interviewer, and anyone involved with counselling (ie all appraisers). The person doing the listening must be active and genuine, that is, they should empathise with the speaker and make appropriate comments.

Motivation. The 'why's' behind people's actions. People behave in certain ways because they have certain needs. These can be basic physiological needs such as the need for food, warmth and shelter, or psychological needs such as companionship, personal growth and self-actualisation. In the work environment it is mainly the psychological needs that require attention as society largely supplies the physiological needs.

Negotiation. Or bargaining. Negotiation concerns the rules of discussion that are involved when two people with differing initial positions try to reach a compromise acceptable to both.

Objectives/targets. Employees perform better when they know what to try and achieve. Targets are often difficult to set. They can be difficult to quantify (especially for managers), or difficult to set at a reasonable level, one neither impossible nor too easy to reach, both of which will demotivate the appraisee.

Peer ratings. These are gaining in popularity though they must be used with caution. They arose because individuals who work together know a great deal about each other's performance. Clearly, they should be used with care. They must be anonymous and confidential. There is the danger that some people might indulge in backbiting and the airing of personal grievances, and try to put each other down in order to show themselves in a better light.

Performance criteria. Some jobs have performance criteria that are simple to determine, eg number of components manufactured in one hour. Others are more difficult, eg the effectiveness of the marketing manager. Whatever the criteria used, it is desirable to choose ones that are objective. If they are quantifiable, all the better.

Person specification. The ideal individual for a particular job.

The specification includes particular categories, such as intelligence, aptitudes, personality. These are derived from the job description and from the individuals who already do the job.

Personality. Relatively permanent ways of behaving which characterise individuals and make them different from others. The differences are called 'traits', eg extroversion, aggression, honesty. Personality, when measured accurately, can be a predictor of job success, and is useful for assessing training needs.

Psychometric testing. A way of collecting personal data that is under-used in the appraisal situation. Psychometric tests and questionnaires can provide detailed, objective, information on abilities, personality and interests very quickly. Tests are accurate predictors of how an individual will perform in various circumstances. For example, they are a particularly useful form of data in appraisals relating to future performance in other roles (promotion/transfer).

Reliability. Any assessment device (eg psychometric test, interview, appraisal system as a whole) should produce consistent, stable findings if used to measure the same thing on two or more occasions.

Selection. Job selection is concerned with picking the right person for the job. Many of the principles of appraisal as outlined in this book apply equally to selection, for instance the need to have accurate and up-to-date job descriptions and person specifications, and ways of accurately assessing candidates on important individual characteristics.

Subordinate ratings. These are another alternative to supervisor ratings, though they may present difficulties and should only be used with care. It is unlikely that subordinates actually know enough about the role of the supervisor to make valid judgements about performance. For this reason, it is usually best to restrict subordinate ratings to areas such as judgement of leadership and social interaction skills.

Supervisor. This broad term means anyone responsible for a group of people (or even a single person) in an organisation. The notion of authority is difficult to assess. In some circumstances the supervisor has a great deal of authority (for example, hiring and firing, discipline), in others very little.

Supervisor ratings. One of the commonest forms of data used in appraisals. They are also one of the most abused assessment techniques. Supervisor ratings scales are often devised without much thought. On the other hand, carefully designed scales provide useful and valid information.

Task analysis. Part of job analysis. The task analysis determines the number and types of tasks involved in the job, the frequency with which they are carried out, and the percentage of time spent on the task.

Training. This is one of the most important outcomes of an appraisal. The analysis of training needs is a crucial part of many appraisals. There is little point in finding out a person's deficiencies if this information isn't acted on, and acted on quickly. The costs of training are usually quickly recouped.

Validation. A good appraisal system will always have defects due to its complexity. Validation is a form of systematic analysis involving experimental analysis of the appraisal system, interviews with the individuals involved, etc, to discover any defects and to find ways of remedying them. Its basic purpose is to minimise the defects.

Validity. The extent to which something (eg the appraisal system, an interview, supervisor ratings) is accurate (is it measuring what it is supposed to measure?) and useful (does it measure or predict performance?) in a particular situation. Validity is often assessed using correlations. A correlation of 1.0 represents perfect validity, while 0.0 represents no validity.

Further Reading

Effective Performance Appraisals, Robert Maddux (Kogan Page, 1987). A brief introductory guide to the subject. Paperback.

How to Employ & Manage Staff, Wendy Wyatt (Northcote House/How To Books, 1990). A practical handbook covering both management practice and the legal requirements of employment statutes and regulations.

How to Manage People at Work, John Humphries (How To Books, 1992). A practical step-by-step guide to everything from motivation and delegation to effective time management.

How to Write a Report, John Bowden (How To Books, 1991). A systematic guide to management report writing and presentation.

Making Performance Appraisals Work, Tom Philp (McGraw-Hill). 1983.

The Secrets of Successful Staff Appraisal and Counselling, Clive Goodworth (Heinemann). 1989.

Performance Appraisal and Career Development, Clive Fletcher & Richard Williams (Hutchinson). 1985. A more detailed and academic study.

Useful Addresses

Advisory, Conciliation and Arbitration Service (ACAS), 27 Wilton Street, London SW1X 2AZ. Tel: (071) 210 3000.

British Association for Commercial & Industrial Education (BACIE), 16 Park Crescent, London W1N 4AP. Tel: (071) 636 5351. BACIE is involved with a key initiative, the **Human Resource Development Partnership**, in association with a number of other leading industrial and training organisations. The Partnership aims to help both organisational and people development for their mutual benefit, focusing on: human resource strategies and planning; developing trainer expertise; preparation for work; promoting the fullest involvement of people in their work; group and team working; self development and continuous development; communications at work; facilitating and managing change; and developing organisational cultures to facilitate the integration of individual and organisational development.

British Education Management & Administration Society (BEMAS), c/o 351 Regents Park Road, Finchley, London N3 1DJ.

British Institute of Management (BIM), Africa House, 64-78 Kingsway, London WC2B 6BL. Tel: (071) 405 3456.

British Psychological Society (BPS), St Andrew's House, 48 Princess Road East, Leicester LE1 7DR. Tel: (0533) 549568.

Career Analysts, Career House, 90 Gloucester Place, London W1H 4BL. Tel: (071) 935 5452.

Centre for Education Management, Danbury Park Management Centre, Danbury, Chelmsford, Essex CM3 4AT. Tel: (0245) 2141.

Commission for Racial Equality, Elliott House, 10/12 Arlington Street, London SW1E 5WH. Tel: (071) 828 7022.

Data Protection Registrar, Springfield House, Water Lane, Wilmslow, Cheshire SK9 5AX. Tel: (0625) 535777.

Department of Employment, Caxton House, Tothill Street, London SW1H 9NF. Tel: (071) 213 3000.

Equal Opportunities Commission, Overseas House, Quay Street, Manchester M3 3HN. Tel: (061) 833 9244.

Health & Safety Inspectorate, Baynards House, 1 Chepstow House, Chepstow Place, London W2 4TF. Tel: (071) 229 3456.

Her Majesty's Stationery Office (HMSO), 49 High Holborn, London WC1V 6HB. Tel: (071) 622 3316.

Industrial Society, Peter Runge House, 3 Carlton House Terrace, London SW1. Tel: (071) 839 4300.

Institute of Administrative Management, 40 Chatsworth Parade, Petts Wood, Orpington, Kent BR5 1RW. Tel: (0689) 75555.

Institute of Management Consultants, 32-33 Hatton Garden, London EC1N 8DL. Tel: (071) 242 1803.

Institute of Personnel Management, IPM House, Camp Road, Wimbledon, London SW19 4UX. Tel: (081) 946 9100.

Institute of Supervisory Management, 22 Bore Street, Lichfield, Staffordshire WS13 6LP. Tel: (0543) 251346.

Institute of Training and Development, Marlow House, Institute Road, Marlow, Buckinghamshire SL7 1BD. Tel: (0628) 890123.

Institution of Industrial Managers, Rochester House, 66 Little Ealing Lane, London W5 4XX. Tel: (081) 579 9411.

National Development Centre for School Management Training, 35 Berkeley Square, Bristol BS8 1JA. Tel: (0272) 303030.

National Examinations Board for Supervisory Studies (NEBSS), 76 Portland Place, London W1N 4AA. Tel: (071) 580 3050.

Women in Management Association, 64 Marryat Road, Wimbledon, London SW19 5BN. Tel: (081) 946 1238.

Index

How to Employ & Manage Staff
Wendy Wyatt

This easy to use handbook will help all managers and supervisors whose work involves them in recruiting and managing staff. Ideal for quick reference, it provides a ready-made framework of modern employment practice from recruitment onwards. It provides a clear account of how to apply the health & safety at work regulations, how to handle record-keeping, staff development, grievance and disciplinary procedures, maternity and sick leave and similar matters for the benefit of the organisation and its employees. The book includes a useful summary of current employment legislation and is complete with a range of model forms, letters, notices and similar documents. Wendy Wyatt GradIPM is a Personnel Management and Employment Consultant; her other books include *Recruiting Success* and *Jobhunt*, and she has contributed regularly to the press on employment matters.
128pp illus. 0 7463 0554 0.

How to Know Your Rights at Work
Robert Spicer MA

Written in clear English, this easy-to-follow handbook sets out everyone's rights at work whether in an office, shop, factory or other setting. It outlines the legal framework, the general duties of employers and employees, the legal scope of 'employment', confidential information, references, being a company director, the contract of employment, pay and deductions, hours of work, absences from work, disciplinary procedures, the ACAS code of practice, the meaning of 'gross misconduct', and grievance procedures.

> 'Justifiably described as a practical guide to employment law. It is clearly written in language readily understood by the layman . . . The text has been well laid out and sections are clearly signposted . . . The extensive use of case study material is interesting and helpful . . . The book is not only relevant to Careers Officers and their clients, but also to other people working in the employment/employment advisory field, eg Citizens Advice Bureaux workers, Personnel officers, Trade Union Personnel, and indeed anyone wishing to find out about their rights at work . . . The sort of book that can be easily dipped into for specific information, but which is interesting enough in its own right to be read from cover to cover.' *Careers Officer Journal.* 'Sets out in simple English everything an employee can expect in today's working environment.'
> *Kent Evening Post.*

Robert Spicer MA(Cantab) is a practising barrister, legal editor and author who specialises in employment law. He was Editor of the Case Index on Employment Law (Kluwer) and has taught law at Bristol University and Bristol Polytechnic.
131pp. 1 85703 009 5.

How to Master Business English
Michael Bennie

Are you communicating effectively? Do your business documents achieve the results you want? Or are they too often ignored or misunderstood? Good communication is the key to success in any business. Whether you are trying to sell a product, answer a query or complaint, or persuade colleagues, the way you express yourself is often as important as what you say. With lots of examples, checklists and questionnaires to help you, this book will speed you on your way, whether as manager, executive, or business student. Contents: Introduction, communication in business, planning, getting the right reaction, the writing process, layout, letters, memos, reports, construction, style, sales letters, letters of complaint, answering complaints, accounts queries, press releases, reports, filing, grammar, punctuation, spelling, glossary, answers to exercises.

> 'An excellent book—not in the least dull . . . Altogether most useful for anyone seeking to improve their communication skills.' *IPS Journal.* 'Gives guidance on writing styles for every situation . . . steers the reader through the principles and techniques of effective letter-writing and document-planning.' *First Voice.* 'Useful chapters on grammar, punctuation and spelling. Frequent questionnaires and checklists enable the reader to check progress.' *Focus (Society of Business Teachers).*

Michael Bennie is a Director of Studies of the Department of Business Writing of Writers College, and author of *How to Do Your Own Advertising* in this series.
£7.99, 208pp illus. 0 7463 0582 6

How to Master Public Speaking
Anne Nicholls

Speaking well in public is one of the most useful skills any of us can acquire. People who can often become leaders in their business, profession or community, and the envy of their friends and colleagues. Whether you are a nervous novice or a practised pro, this step-by-step handbook tells you everything you need to know to master this highly prized communication skill. Contents: Preface, being a skilled communicator, preparation, researching your audience, preparing a speech, finding a voice, body language and non-verbal communication, dealing with nerves, audiovisual aids, the physical environment, putting it all together on the day, audience feedback, dealing with the media, glossary, further reading, useful contacts, index. Anne Hulbert Nicholls BA(Hons) PGCE was a Lecturer in Communications and Journalism in a College of Education for 14 years and ran courses in Presentation Skills and Effective Speaking for local business people. She now runs seminars and conferences for a publishing company and writes articles for a number of national magazines and newspapers. Her articles appear regularly in *Living* magazine. She has also worked in Public Relations and for BBC Radio.
160pp illus. 0 7463 0521 4

How to Write a Report
John Bowden

Communicating effectively on paper is an essential skill for today's business or professional person. Good report-writing is a highly effective means of achieving a wide range of objectives, for example in managing an organisation, dealing with staffing, sales and marketing, production, computer operations, financial planning and reporting, feasibility studies and business innovation. Written by an experienced manager and staff trainer, this well-presented handbook provides a very clear step-by-step framework for every individual, whether dealing with professional colleagues, customers, clients, suppliers or junior or senior staff.

'Most of us have need to write a report of some kind at various times, and this book has real value. In the chapter entitled "Some common types of Report" 23 different types are discussed and hints given for their compilation and presentation, followed by a checklist to ensure the writer does not overlook any point. The choice of paper, covers and binding is the topic of another chapter as well as the use of illustrations. Teachers will be pleased to know that language has not been forgotten, and the items covered in this section are style, punctuation and common errors to be avoided. A thoroughly commendable book.' *IPS Journal*.

John Bowden BSc(Econ) MSc studied at the London School of Economics. He has long experience both as a professional manager in industry, and as a Senior Lecturer running courses in accountancy, auditing, and effective communication, up to senior management level.
160pp illus. 1 85703 035 4.

How to Pass That Interview
Judith Johnstone

Everyone knows how to shine at interview—or do they? When every candidate becomes the perfect clone of the one before, you have to have that extra 'something' to raise your chances about the rest. Using a systematic and practical approach, this new How To book takes you step-by-step through the essential pre-interview groundwork, the interview encounter itself, and what you can learn from the experience afterwards. The book contains sample pre- and post-interview correspondence, and is complete with a guide to further reading, glossary of terms, and index. Judith Johnstone has written extensively on employment-related subjects. A Graduate of the Institute of Personnel Management, she has been an instructor in Business Studies and adult literacy tutor, and has long experience of helping people at work.
128pp illus. 1 85703 004 4

How to Keep Business Accounts
Peter Taylor
Second Edition

A new revised edition of an easy-to-understand handbook for all business owners and managers.

> 'Will help you sort out the best way to carry out double entry book-keeping, as well as providing a clear step-by-step guide to accounting procedures.' *Mind Your Own Business.* 'Progresses through the steps to be taken to maintain an effective double entry book-keeping system with the minimum of bother.' *The Accounting Technician.* 'Compulsory reading.' *Manager, National Westminster Bank (Midlands).*

Peter Taylor is a Fellow of the Institute of Chartered Accountants, and of the Chartered Association of Certified Accountants. He has many years' practical experience of advising small businesses.
176pp illus. 0 7463 0618 0

How to Master Book-Keeping
Peter Marshall

Book-Keeping can seem a confusing subject for people coming to it for the first time. This very clear book will be welcomed by everyone wanting a really user-friendly guide to recording business transactions step-by-step. Illustrated at every stage with specimen entries, the book will also be an ideal companion for students taking LCCI, RSA, BTEC, accountancy technician and similar courses at schools, colleges or training centres. Typical business transactions are used to illustrate all the essential theory, practice and skills required to be effective in a real business setting. Contents: Preface, introduction, theory of double entry, day books, cash book, bank reconciliation, petty cash book, journal, postage book, the ledger, discounts, control accounts, trial balance, accruals and prepayments, revenue accounts, the balance sheet, manufacturing accounts, depreciation, bad and doubtful debts, partnership and accounts, amalgamation of sole proprietorships into a partnership, limited companies, 'going limited', reflection, club accounts, asset disposals, correction of errors, VAT accounts, incomplete records, interpretation of accounts, wages, stock records. Peter Marshall BSc(Econ) BA(Hons) FRSA FSTB MBIM has been Tutor in Education at the University of Lancaster and Director of Studies at the Careers College, Cardiff. He has contributed regularly to *FOCUS on Business Education*
176pp illus. 1 85703 022 2.

How to Raise Business Finance
Peter Ibbetson

Every business needs to raise money from time to time. It may be for start-up capital, to cover a difficult cash flow, to invest in research and development, to finance new equipment, premises, or exports, or to retructure the business as a whole. Written by a professional banker, this highly readable book explains what finance costs, what base rates and APR means, how fixed interest loans work. It discusses where cash can be found in a business, for example from existing debtors/creditors, as well as outside lenders. It considers the importance of the balance sheet, track record, gearing, overheads, project viability, and the importance of cash flow forecasting (explaining why this may differ markedly from profit forecasts). Equity financing and management buyouts are explained too, and the role of financial institutions and government sources summarised. Whole chapters are devoted to special forms of finance such as leasing, factoring, contract hire, and finance for exporters, backed up with pages of key references, contacts and addresses, and a helpful glossary of financial and banking terms.

'Gives the right amount of information.' *Association of British Chambers of Commerce.* 'A lucid account of the steps by which a small businessman can substantially strengthen his case.' *The Financial Times.*

Peter Ibbetson is an Associate of the Chartered Institute of Bankers, and an author and broadcaster on banking matters.
160pp illus. 07463 0338 6

How to Invest in Stocks and Shares
Dr John White

This book has been specially prepared to help and guide those with a substantial sum to invest (often more than £50,000) and who are considering investing all or part of this sum in quoted securities. Often such investors have such a sum as a result of a recent inheritance, for example when the house of a deceased parent has been sold. This new book recognises that such investors are not normally interested in suspect get-rich-quick schemes, but rather in a practical and level-headed approach in which longterm objectives are important. This book therefore provides a complete step-by-step framework to share selection and dealing, and portfolio management, against a background of longer term trends. Dr John White, an Oxford graduate, is himself an experienced investor and adviser to an investment company. He has a professional background in computers and has produced a range of software for chart analysis.
192pp illus. 1 85703 036 2

How to Start a Business from Home
Graham Jones
Second Edition

Most people have dreamed of starting their own business from home at some time or other; but how do you begin? What special skills do you need? This great value-for-money paperback has the answers, showing how you can profit from your own talents and experience, and start turning spare time into cash from the comfort of your own home. *How to Start a Business From Home* contains a wealth of ideas, projects, tips, facts, checklists and quick-reference information for everyone—whether in between jobs, taking early retirement, or students and others with time to invest. Packed with information on everything from choosing a good business idea and starting up to advertising, book-keeping and dealing with professionals, this book is essential reading for every budding entrepreneur.

'Full of ideas and advice.' *The Daily Mirror.*

Graham Jones BSc(Hons) is an editor, journalist and lecturer specialising in practical business subjects. His other books include *Fit to Manage* and *The Business of Freelancing.*
176pp, 1 85703 012 5

How to Do Your Own Advertising
Michael Bennie

'Entrepreneurs and small businesses are flooding the market with new products and services; the only way to beat the competition is successful selling—and that means advertising.' But what can you afford? This book is for anyone who needs—or wants—to advertise effectively, but does not want to pay agency rates. It will also be useful to those who simply want to know what is involved in advertising, whether as students, business people or interested laymen. What are the secrets of putting together effective ads? Even the basic design can be done by someone with a little imagination and creatively. This book shows you step-by- step how to assemble a simple, straightforward, yet highly successful ad or brochure with the minimum of outside help. Every step is clearly explained with the beginner in mind. There are numerous illustrations, lots of examples of actual ads, a variety of case studies to show the principles in practice and the aim throughout is to make advertising easy and enjoyable. Complete with questionnaires and checklists to help you check your progress. Michael Bennie has had many years' professional experience as a Sales Manager with a number of international companies, covering all aspects of sales and copywriting. He is now a freelance copywriter and advertising consultant, and Director of Studies at the Copywriting School.
176pp illus. 0 7463 0579 6